THE FOURTEENTH SUMMER

Gary Paulsen is the distinguished author of numerous books, ranging from Westerns to DIY. He has received great acclaim and many awards for his novels written for young people. *Hatchet* and its sequel, *The Return*, are among his best-known works. He has also written *Tasting the Thunder*, *The Fourteenth Summer*, and *Night-john*, all available from Macmillan Children's Books.

He lives with his family in New Mexico, USA. He has sailed the Pacific and competed in the gruelling 1,049 mile Iditarod dog-sled race across Alaska.

Also by Gary Paulsen

THE FOURTEENTH SUMMER

Gary Paulsen

MACMILLAN

CHILDREN'S BOOKS

First published 1992 by Delacorte Press
in the United States of America under the
Title of The Haymeadow

This edition published 1996 by Macmillan Children's Books
a division of Macmillan Publishers Ltd
25 Eccleston Place, London SW1W 9NF

Associated companies throughout the world

5 7 9 8 6 4

ISBN 0-330-33006-3

Phototypeset by Intype London Ltd
Printed and bound in Great Britain by
Mackays of Chatham PLC, Chatham, Kent

To the Burks,
Lynn, Tami, Alex, Justin, and Brian

CHAPTER ONE

John Barron was fourteen years old.

Just.

Yesterday, he thought – I was fourteen yesterday and nothing changed. He wasn't sure what he wanted to change, or how it should change, or even why it should change but he wanted something to change and nothing had and he felt cheated.

He stopped halfway between the house and horse barn and smelled the air, looked at the mountains to the west. It was early summer and summers in Wyoming were hot but it hadn't been hot yet and he wondered if rain would break the cool spell and bring hot weather.

They said weather came from the mountains and it smelled of rain and maybe it would change things.

There it was again, he thought – change. Why did he want it to change? Heat made the sheep stink more and die more and get sick more and they weren't up in the mountains yet – why hope for heat? Four dogs, drawn by the sound of the screen door slamming, came running from in back of the barn. They were border collies – named Pete, Billy, Jenny, and Peg – for working the sheep. They climbed on John and he petted them and ruffled their hair.

He scratched where something had bitten the back of Peg's neck – blackfly, mosquito, tick, or all of them. Once petted the dogs swirled around him, made dust, and were gone.

John was wearing jeans and cowboy boots and a denim shirt and a straw summer western hat and when he lifted the hat there was a white line where the hat kept the sun from burning. The rest of his face was past burned, past tanned – looked like brown leather. He had wide blue eyes and a straight mouth.

He looked exactly like his father. Who was also named John Barron. Who looked like his father had looked when he was young and his father who had started the ranch where they still lived.

The Barron spread, they called it.

They said the old man, dead for thirty years, had come west with a gun and two horses.

'He was mean,' John's father had told him on one of the rare occasions when they talked. 'Meaner than nine hells. He just said, this is mine, and nobody dared argue . . .'

He had claimed nine hundred and sixty thousand acres of Wyoming with nothing but that gun and two horses and a half-broken saddle and made the claim stick, made the Barron spread his and all his.

Then he sent back east for a mail-order bride. Her name was Emma and she tamed him some and then turned as tough as him. She had John's grandfather in the back of the chuckwagon during roundup, was out one day having the baby, and then went back to cooking for the hands and kept John's grandfather in an old dynamite box next to the stove.

The wagon was still there, next to the barn, dried and weathered and not used but sitting there.

All of this John knew. All of this he'd been told and told again, to be proud of it, to know it and take pride in it because it was family pride and that was the only kind of pride to have.

Even though it was all gone.

The ranch was called the Three Bar S now and had all sheep and was owned lock, stock, and barrel by eastern corporations who had taken it over when banks had foreclosed during the Great Depression because John's grandfather had made bad loans and didn't understand how to save money and be mean the way *his* father had been.

The family was still there. They had never left. The corporations hired them to run the ranch, paid the family to stay and take care of things – to be caretakers on their own place. But they owned nothing, the Barrons.

And we're supposed to be proud, John thought, looking at the old wagon where his grandfather had been born.

Proud.

Of nothing. Of being fourteen. Of nothing.

'Hey kid, where's your old man?'

John looked to the corral in back of the barn where Cawley was working with a horse. Cawley was one of two permanent hired hands – the other was an old man named Tinckner. Horace Cawley – always called just Cawley – had been with the ranch since before John was born, was probably about thirty-five, skinny with sloping shoulders and almost a perfect half-circle bitten out of the top of his right ear from a bar fight at a rodeo in Cheyenne years before.

'Town,' John said. 'He's gone to town until evening – left early this morning with Tink.'

'Damn.' Cawley was leaning against the corral fence – three-inch steel pipes welded to uprights to make a steel circle eighty feet across. He spit tobacco juice in the dust.

'What's the matter?'

'I was going to work on that truck today but I need plugs and a new fan belt. I should have told him to get the stuff in town.'

'Did he know about the truck?'

'Yeah. We talked about it last night.'

'Then he'll probably remember to get plugs and stuff on his own.'

'We need the truck to pull the trailer up to the haymeadow . . .'

John nodded but said nothing and Cawley went back to work.

The truck was little more than a frame with a motor on it – an old 1951 GMC half-ton with the box gone and chains on the rear wheels. It only ran once a year, to pull the trailer up to the haymeadow.

The haymeadow.

John smiled when he thought of it. The haymeadow was in a valley up in the mountains where the Barrons had always summered their cattle. It was four sections – four square miles – of sweet grass between two ridges of peaks, all at and above timberline. With the cattle gone and the ranch in sheep every summer they took the sheep up there and Tinckner would stay in the small shepherd's trailer – something like a covered wagon with rubber wheels that the old truck pulled up every summer – until it was fall and time to bring them down before the winter storms hit.

Almost three months the old man stayed alone with the sheep and the four dogs and once John had asked him if it wasn't lonely up there, with just the sheep.

'Got the dogs,' Tinks said.

'Well then, lonely with just the sheep and the dogs.'

'Got the mountains.'

And John knew that if he kept asking it would just keep going. Got the mountains. Got the trees. Got the rocks. Got the elk . . .

John had quit asking. Tinckner didn't like to talk much and sometimes went days without saying anything at all except to whistle at the dogs. Short whistles that meant go left, go right, take the sheep out or bring them in; all command whistles. John knew some of the whistles, or knew how to do them, but there were many of them he didn't know. Tinckner could send two dogs out to bring in two sheep, open a gate, close a gate, then separate the two sheep and bring one in to shear – all with whistles.

The dogs were part of him, almost knew what he was thinking.

Chores, John thought – he couldn't stand around and think all day. There were chores to do. He had to clean the barn, clip hooves on two horses, then start stocking the trailer for Tinckner.

He smelled the air again. Rain.

Maybe it would change things.

CHAPTER TWO

John barely remembered his mother. Long, dark hair and
a smile. He was three when she died. She loved to ride
and had a horse come over on her backward and she lived
for a week and then was not alive anymore and he didn't
know much of her except pictures that his father kept and
now John wasn't sure if he remembered her at all or just
thought he did from the pictures.

He knew his father had loved her. No, that wasn't
right either. He still loved her. He had never remarked,
though there had been several opportunities.

'He beat the horse,' Cawley had said one, sitting
drinking Canadian whiskey out of a small bottle next to
the bunkhouse. 'With his hands. I couldn't stop him. He
beat the horse to death. It broke his hands to do it and I
couldn't stop him.'

Once a month John's father went to her grave twenty-
three miles away near the Sidown Baptist Church that
wasn't a church anymore but just a graveyard out in the

middle of nowhere, on a bluff above a valley. She had loved mountains, his father said, and you could see the mountains from the grave site, spread out wide and beautiful, and he thought she would want to be there even though they weren't Baptists or anything else, for that matter. Once a month he went there and cleaned the grave and put fresh plastic flowers in a small brass vase bolted to the granite stone.

CYNTHIA BARRON
Died in Full Beauty

And the date. He would bring a thermos of coffee and sit and talk to her, tell her things that had happened and once he had brought John to spend the day. John tried to understand but it all seemed vague and after sitting staring at the stone trying to remember her, trying to separate the memories from the pictures he'd seen and the things his father had told him, his mind drifted and he didn't hear.

His father had not taken him again but still went, once a month, and everybody at the ranch was glad he did.

'It calms him,' Cawley said. 'You need that with him. They've all needed that, the Barrons – calming. There's that wild blood, that wilding blood in you that needs taming now and again. You'll need it too.'

John worked all morning. It took him twenty minutes each to clip the hooves on the two horses – it reminded him of cutting fingernails whenever he did it. One was a mare named Speck and the other a large sorrel gelding named Spud. They were the same age – eleven – and had been his horses, the ones he usually rode, for at least six years. Altogether he didn't know how many horses the ranch had. Sometimes the rich people from the corporation would bring in twenty or thirty – some of them plugs, some good – just to keep them. But the steady herd John thought must be over a hundred. Cawley took care of the horses – he wouldn't work with sheep except to help in lambing and shearing and when they moved them to the high country.

'I hate 'em,' he said, and John agreed with him.

'They're stupid and all they do is blow snot all over your legs when you walk through them and stink and die for no damn reason. Cattle maybe ain't much, but they beat sheep solid when it comes to brains . . .'

Cutting their hooves was just a matter of getting the clippers and bringing Spud and Speck into the stall. They've done it so many times they would practically lean against the wall and raise each hoof to be clipped.

He trimmed them evenly, mostly so he wouldn't be embarrassed when Al Spencer came to shoe them. Al came every year in late spring or early summer to shoe the horses they were going to use. They let the horses run shoeless all winter in the low country but the ones they used to drive the sheep into the high country – to the haymeadow – had to have shoes to be able to take the rocks. If the hooves were ragged when Al came to shoe them – he was due tomorrow – he could chew on John for it and John would rather avoid the chewing.

Like black butter, the hooves cut. They trimmed in neat little snicks, then he used a rasp to even them off – even though Al would do it again when he came, even them around the shoes so they fit well.

When he was done John gave each of the horses a small handful of oats – they would get their regular ration later in the day – and turned them in back of the barn with the other horses pulled in for the drive into the high country.

He loved the drive into the mountains. The sheep were slow and they went down road only with persistent coaxing and pushing. It took a week to make the drive, riding in the smell of them – ammonia from their urine, oily lanolin that made everything taste bitter from their skin and the short wool, not grown much after spring shearing. Then there were the flies, hordes of them biting and stinging, swarming on the sheep and horses and dogs and him. Still, it always reminded John of what it must have been like to drive cattle in the old days. He had never done it – his whole life the ranch had been in sheep and he had only been on five drives. But driving cattle, just the words – *cattle drive* – seemed to draw him.

He had read about it – everything he could get his hands on. And watched old movies. They had a satellite dish and received close to two hundred channels. And he'd learned some from the movies and much more from books but he still could only imagine it. Living in the saddle that way.

His great-grandfather, it was said, kept a horse saddled by the house all the time – even at night while he was sleeping – and wouldn't walk even to the outhouse to go to the bathroom. There were many legends about him – some of them true. He'd ridden out the front of a stampede, ridden them out and turned them when another man would have run for his life or died, stomped into mush.

The barn needed only minor cleaning and he did it with the wheelbarrow and shovel and the thought came while he was scooping up horse manure. A nudge thought.

His great-grandfather wouldn't have cleaned the barn, wouldn't have gone to sheep, wouldn't have – wouldn't have been too busy for his son.

There.

The thought had come before. Not so much a year or two ago, but more often now, and not always when he really expected it except that it sometimes came when he was doing something he didn't like.

When he was studying. He hated studying and had to work at it and his father made him do it and his grades were all right but he didn't like it and sometimes the thought came then: The old man would have spent more time with his son.

Or during lambing. They had to be ready twenty-four hours a day when the lambs came and it took about a week and a half and the whole world seemed to be made of stink and afterbirth and dead lambs and dead sheep and that led right into shearing, so that everybody worked until he dropped every night and John hated it and the thought would come then: He wouldn't have kept so much to himself, would have talked more to his son, his blood.

The problem was, he didn't really know one way or the other what his great-grandfather would have done.

He didn't know that much about him.

CHAPTER THREE

At noon John went into the kitchen and made a sandwich with peanut butter, lunch meat, grape jelly, and a sliced pickle – he'd learned it from Jimmy Cranney, a friend in school. Jimmy went to the same school but lived nearly forty-five miles away, so during the school year they were best friends and come summer they just about didn't see each other. Jimmy's place was small – about six hundred acres – and they raised Appaloosa horses to sell. Which wasn't cattle either, John thought, but then again it wasn't sheep.

They did all their own cooking at the ranch – which meant they ate mostly out of cans because usually there was too much work going to come in and cook – and John took the sandwich and a glass of milk up to his room.

His room was the top, back room in the two-storey ranch house. It was not the original Barron house – that had been a log house and burned down under mysterious circumstances before even John's grandfather was

born – but had been built around 1900. It was frame
construction with white-painted wood boards for the walls
and the only thing John liked about it was the view. He
could sit in his room and look out the window and see the
mountains. He had a small desk there – an old wooden
table, really – and he sat at the desk and ate the sandwich
and looked at the mountains while he chewed.

When he was done he cleaned the crumbs and
dumped them in a small cardboard box he used for a
wastebasket and started back out of the room but stopped
and looked at the poster on the wall.

There were four pictures of his great-grandfather
made during his entire life – that's all. Four. And John
had made blowups of them and had a photographic studio
in Cheyenne make a larger poster with the four pictures on
it, and he could not come into the room without stopping to
look at them.

It was like looking at himself.

The resemblance was more than striking – it was
uncanny. Even John's father noted it. At the same studio
in Cheyenne – more as a joke than anything else – John
had ordered an old-time photograph of himself, done with
a floppy old cowboy hat and a broken Winchester the
photographer had there for props. The picture was shot
in black and white with a slightly fuzzy focus and he had
taped it on the wall next to the poster.

It looked exactly the same. The same slight droop to
the left eyelid, the same straight nose, the same set to the
shoulders and eyes that looked dead out into the camera.
He could have put it in any of the pictures on the poster
and it would have fit perfectly except that his great-grand-

father had been older in the pictures and had some marks of age – weathered lines in his face and scruffier, torn clothes.

And the gun.

In every picture he was wearing a gun, an old Colt single-action .45-caliber with smooth wooden grips in a worn, oiled cartridge belt and holster. John did not carry a gun but he had seen the gun owned by his great-grand-father. John's father had it in a wooden box, along with the old man's chaps – scarred and ripped – and a pair of his work gloves. They had the ends of the fingers cut off so he could feel the rope or use the gun easily.

It was heavy, the gun, and it didn't look heavy in any of the pictures. John had picked it up, hefted it, aimed it and it must have weighed close to four pounds, maybe five with the cartridge belt full of shells and the holster. Five pounds on one hip his whole life and yet except to go to bed he was said never to take if off and when he finally grew so old – he made ninety-two, if the records were accurate – that they had to put him in a nursing home he took the gun with him. And kept it. They were nervous about it in the home and removed the firing pin but he kept the gun and it was hanging next to his head the night he died in 1954.

John had studied the poster so long he'd memorized everything on it and yet he stopped every time he came into the room and looked at it and wondered what it would have been like if *he* had lived then and somehow had known the old man when he was young and had only the gun and two horses and all that land before the eastern corporations took it . . .

He shook his head and left the room. There was work to do still and he put his hat on and went outside, was walking across the open space leading to the barn when he saw the dust.

From the yard and house area, which was on a slight rise, it was possible to see the mile and a half to the main road – it was low, rolling hills of grass with small rocky outcroppings – and he saw that a vehicle had turned off the main road and was coming toward the ranch. It left a plume of dust and for a moment he couldn't recognize it. Then it crested a rise and he saw the dark blue of the ranch pickup.

'They're coming back early,' Cawley called. He'd seen the dust as well and was leaning on the rail of the corral. 'I'll bet he didn't get the plugs and belt . . .'

John shrugged. 'I don't know.' It was strange for his father to come back early. The trip to town took close to an hour and a half, one way, and he didn't like to waste it. Usually he did it once and stayed all day rather than have to make another trip soon.

He watched the truck and when it was still over a quarter-mile away he saw that his father was alone.

'Where's Tink?' Cawley asked. 'Your old man is alone.'

John said nothing but stood and waited while his father drove into the yard and stopped the truck next to him. Cawley had come from the corral and the dust cloud that followed the truck settled over them.

John's father stepped from the truck.

'Where's Tink?' Cawley asked.

John's father spit and looked past the barn to the lambing pens but he wasn't seeing anything. They were empty – all the sheep and lambs were off on the west side of the ranch in a four-hundred-acre pasture. Being held so they could be more easily started on the drive to the mountains.

'Tink's not coming back,' he said after a moment.

'Not coming back?' John asked. 'Why?'

'He's got a cancer. They've got to do more tests on him but the doc told me he thought it was all through him and the tests would just confirm it.' He was still looking at the lambing pens, as if something very important were out there. 'I've got to go back. They're going to try some different ways to fix it and I should be there. It don't look so good.'

'Damn.' Cawley rubbed his neck. 'Old Tink . . . damn.'

'I don't know how long I'll be. I'll stay with him until . . . well, until it doesn't matter. The doc says if the therapy doesn't work it will go fast but it might be two weeks or a month or even longer before it ends. I can come home now and again but I should be there as much as I can.'

'But what about the drive up to the haymeadow?' Cawley asked. John was thinking about Tinckner. How he did things – the way he looked putting snoose in his lower lip. The way he smiled. Gone.

'Tink worked here man and boy,' John's father said. 'He worked with my father, John's grandfather, and knew his great-grandfather. We're his family and I can't let him rot alone.'

Rot, John thought – he was going to rot. Old Tink. God.

'I know,' Cawley said. 'I wasn't arguing with you. I just meant what about it?'

'You and the boy.' John's father looked at him. 'You

and John take them up – you can do it. Then you come back down and John stays with the sheep.'

'Me?' John said. 'Alone?'

Yes, John thought, and the sheep and the mountains and the coyotes and the bears and and and. 'I don't know what to do – how to do it.' *He* wouldn't do it, he thought – not the old man. It slipped in. A quick thought.

'There's nothing to know. You take the dogs and you take care of the sheep. I did it when I was fifteen and you can do it. Cawley has to be here to run the ranch – the folks from back east are coming and we have to be ready for them – and I have to spend time with Tink.'

'I'll take him up there,' Cawley said. 'Don't worry about it. We'll talk as we go and he'll be fine – hell, you were, weren't you? He's as good as you.'

The two men smiled and John's father left them, went into the house and was out in three minutes with his shaving kit and a paper sack with magazines.

'Tink likes the stockman magazines,' he said, dumping the sack and the kit on the seat of the truck.

'What he really likes is *Playboy*,' Cawley said.

'Not in the hospital.' John's father climbed into the truck. 'In the hospital he likes the stockman magazines . . .'

He nodded to John and wheeled the truck and drove away – not fifteen minutes had passed since he arrived – and John watched him drive away until it was just the dust out by the main road. he watched until even the dust was gone, settling back, then he turned toward the barn.

Well, he thought.

You wanted a change.

CHAPTER FOUR

He sat in his room that night and started a list:

    Gun
    Food
    Sleeping Gear
    Four pairs of socks
    Four pairs of underwear
    Two shirts
    Three pairs of jeans
    Toothbrush
    Three months

The last thing on the list seemed to write itself. Three months. He was going to be alone with the sheep for the rest of June, July, and August, until the first week in September.

I'll go crazy, he thought. Nuts. I don't even know what to do, how to do anything. How can Cawley teach me? Seven, eight days and he's supposed to teach me how to take care of six thousand sheep for three months?

He threw the pencil down, looked out the window at the mountains. It wasn't the range he could see but the next one, the next one over where they had to take the sheep, but he visualized it in his mind.

The large meadow, huge, surrounded by peaks, and in all the vastness the small trailer and him. Just him.

And the dogs, of course.

And the sheep.

And the mountains.

The day had started wrong, with the sad news about Tink, and it hadn't seemed to get better.

John's father had gone back to town promising to come back to the ranch with plugs and belt and to pick up the list for provisions the next morning. John had to have the list ready by then.

After that he and Cawley had gone to work on the wagon. It wintered next to the old granary – a building made of logs hand-hewn by John's great-grandfather. The wagon sat there without moving so that the tires had gone flat and needed pumping with the hand pump and then Cawley decided they should grease the bearings, which meant pulling each wheel and repacking it with the thick wheel-bearing grease they kept in a bucket hanging in the granary and by three o'clock John was grease to his eyeballs.

Then they had to restretch and retie the canvas top to the wagon and clean the stove – a small wood-burning stove in the corner of the trailer – and while they were cleaning the stove Cawley went to the barn for something and John was left alone in the trailer.

He had been in it before, of course, many times. But never to stay.

Never to stay for three months and he looked at it differently now. It was tiny – six feet wide, twelve feet long, with a bunk and wooden boxes nailed sideways to the wooden side to make shelves and a Coleman lantern hanging from the center bow that held the canvas up.

Tiny.

The mattress smelled, well, like Tink and on his best day Tink didn't smell good. Even if they aired it out the smell would be there and the thought of three months sleeping in the little wagon on the stinky bed ...

On the side of the wagon, just below where the canvas top started up, there was a calendar sheet nailed up, the kind with all the months laid out in squares and next to the calendar there was a stub of a wooden pencil tied hanging on a string. The three months for last year – when Tink had done it last – were marked off a day at a time, each day with a small X and each month with lines through the X's to mark the end of the month.

So Tink hadn't liked it that much either, or why would he have kept track of each day?

They had worked on the trailer all day and the thought of summering in at the haymeadow with the sheep didn't seem to get any easier to handle.

They stripped it out, aired the mattress, used a hose to clean the box of the wagon until it was fresh and new, and when they were done Cawley shook his head.

'Let's let her dry until tomorrow, then we'll start loading her up.'

They had eaten canned chili and crackers for dinner

and John had come up to this room to do the list while Cawley sat down below in the living room watching reruns of *Bonanza*, which he loved.

Dog food.

God, he'd almost forgotten dog food. Let's see, four dogs, a pound a dog a day, four pounds a day, say thirty pounds a week, a hundred and twenty pounds a month, three hundred and sixty pounds of dog food.

Three hundred and sixty pounds of dog food. Where would he keep it?

He went back to the list.

> Dog food
> Batteries (for the flashlight)
> First-aid kit
> First-aid kit for the dogs
> Feed for the horse

He stopped writing and leaned back. Downstairs he heard the phone ring and thought it was his father, but Cawley got it and didn't call him down so it was probably some corporation business.

His eyes fell on the poster and some of the stories came to his mind.

Stories about the old man, the first John Barron. About how mean he was, how tough he was – none of the stories talked about humour or anything happy. Only about mean and tough.

There was a bad man who came to the territory at one point, just bad. He killed a rancher and made off with his wife and when he was done killed her and they'd gone after the man with a posse – more a group of ranchers – but hadn't caught him. John Barron the first declined to ride with the posse and they made fun of him for that, thinking he was afraid but it wasn't that.

He went alone and he found the man and killed him and skinned some of him and kept the head and used the skin for a vest and part of the skull for a button bowl and the vest and bowl were on display in a museum in Cheyenne if anybody doubted it.

Mean. Nobody ever found the rest of the body because he dragged it out in a gully and let the coyotes have it.

He used that gun, John thought, looking at the poster. He killed the man with the gun I held and then skinned him with those same hands that are holding the reins of the horse in that picture.

He thought suddenly of Tink. He'd known John Barron the first – known him and spoke to him and knew more about him than anybody else. John had always meant to sit down with Tink and ask him, talk to him, find out more about his great-grandfather but Tink had never been close to anybody – not even John's father. He slept alone in the old bunkhouse, even though Cawley slept in the house with John and his father.

Had slept, John thought. Tink had slept in the bunkhouse.

He felt a sadness about the old man, about Tink, but he had never really known him. Just seen him working, or sitting, or tending sheep. There never seemed a right time to sit and ask him anything, and now it was too late.

He shook his head and stood. It was early yet, just getting dark, but he had to get up early and he stripped for bed and dropped his clothes on the chair by the desk under the windows.

With the light out he could see the glow from the

moon and he opened the window and lay on the bed without covers, letting the cool evening come over him.

Outside, one of the dogs barked – he couldn't tell which one – and he heard several coyotes answer it.

Sleep came slowly, and all the way down he thought of Tink and how he had missed the chance to talk to him.

CHAPTER FIVE

John awakened slowly, opening his eyes last, when the rest of him was full awake. There was just a smoky bit of light coming in the window. Dawn. It must be about four-thirty. And quiet outside. They had had chickens for a while, and a rooster that crowed them awake, but the dogs herded anything they could – sometimes tried to turn birds flying over the yard or water running out the over-flow on the stock tank – and they kept herding the chickens into a small group, worrying them and pushing them around the yard until a couple of them died and his father got rid of the rest.

But as he shoved his legs down into the cold tube of his jeans he heard a meadowlark sing, then another answered him and then he heard Cawley come out on the porch and hawk and spit and he knew another day had started. He smiled, thinking of Cawley. He'd made fun of Tink once for staying in the old bunkhouse when he could have had a room in the main house. But after they'd put in a septic and had running water and a good bathroom Cawley still went outside to spit.

'You spit in dirt,' he'd said to John's father. 'Not in some bowl of water in a special room in the house. Besides, it wasn't any part of hiring on, you telling me where to spit . . .'

Two days had passed since John's father had come home with the news about Tink.

John pulled his socks and the pointed-toe boots on and went downstairs with his shirt on but still open. He splashed water in his face, dried on the towel that had been hanging in the bathroom for going on a month, and went into the kitchen.

Cawley had opened two cans of corned beef hash, emptied each one on a separate plate and was frying eggs in lard on the stove. When the eggs were crinkled and starting to burn he dropped two of them – the yolks still runny with the whites not quite cooked on top – on each pile of cold hash.

'Eat. We start up today and we won't have much for lunch. This will stick to you.'

John looked at his place. The uncooked egg white looked just like the boogers that were always hanging out of little Davey Haller's nose on the bus.

'What's the matter?'

'Nothing.' Maybe, he thought, if I jam it all down into the hash and eat it without looking or thinking about it. He used his fork to mash the eggs down and mix them in with the hash and then tried a mouthful. The hash was cold and at least half grease and the lard on the eggs turned hard with it hit the cold hash and he ate without looking. Just take a mouthful and swallow, he thought, then another. It'll go down. He thought of the day before while he was eating.

It had been one of those disasters that maybe turned out for the better. Cawley had decided to start the old GMC even though he didn't have new plugs and belts, just to see if it would run, and it promptly threw a rod and started hammering and bouncing.

'Well,' he said. 'That tears it.'

'What about using the ranch pickup?' John had asked.

'Your dad needs it. No, we'll have to do it the old-fashioned way.'

John had thought the old GMC *was* the old-fashioned way. It was the only way he'd ever seen them pull the wagon up.

But Cawley showed him a long piece of wood with a bolt hole through one end out by the side of the barn. It had been there as long as John had known things but he just thought it was an old piece of wood.

'Wagon tongue,' Cawley said. 'White oak – lasts forever.' He went to a pile of junk in the granary and found other pieces of wood and bolts and chains and then, from the wall of the granary, harnesses.

'You're going to pull the wagon all the way up there with horses?'

Cawley had looked at him in surprise. 'Sure. That's how we always did it. Trucks is a new idea . . .'

'But we don't have workhorses,' John said. 'We just have riding horses.'

Cawley smiled. 'They'll drive just fine. Don't worry about it. We'll harness Spud and Speck today on some weight and you'll see how they do. There won't be no problems.'

John had doubted it but Cawley had been right. They brought the mare and gelding out of the corral, let them smell the harnesses and collars, then harnessed them up. They both stood quietly while Cawley finished harnessing, though Speck – she was always curious – looked around at the contraption on her back for a moment. John helped Cawley back them into position, one on each side of the tongue, and they hooked the trace chains to the doubletrees, snapped the tongue crosspiece up to the collars, and they still stood quietly.

Cawley climbed into the seat of the wagon, John sat next to him, and Cawley slapped them lightly on the rump with the lines.

That did it.

They slammed forward so hard, John went over the seat backward and landed inside the wagon and Cawley had all he could do to hold them while they took out across the prairie.

They calmed down after a bit, snorted some, then went to work and in ten or fifteen minutes acted like they'd been pulling wagons forever.

'Slick as a wet cat,' Cawley had said. 'We'll throw your saddle in the back and you'll have two horses up there to use.'

I won't get lonely, John thought, looking at the empty plate, wondering how he'd eaten it all without throwing up. I'll have the horses and the dogs and the sheep and the mountains and and and . . .

After easing Spud and Speck into driving instead of

riding they spent the rest of the day getting ready. Cawley brought out a box of shoes and tools and shoed both Speck and Spud because they wouldn't be here when the farrier came. John had never seen him shoe before – other than to repair a problem shoe if it came loose – and he was surprised at how well Cawley did it.

'How come you don't shoe all of them?' he asked. Cawley was putting the tools away and he turned after setting the toolbox on the shelf.

'Because I didn't hire on to shoe horses. I hired on to hand, and that's it. Being a hand don't mean shoeing a whole herd of horses come summer every year. Now, let's load that wagon.'

John's list was nothing compared to what Cawley put in for him. Cans and more cans of food – he stripped the house, which was always full of canned food.

'Can't have nothing much fresh,' Cawley said. 'It'll go on you right away. We could have tried some of that freeze-dried stuff you just boil with water and you wouldn't have empty cans to carry back in the fall. But Tink, he don't trust that dried stuff, wanted canned goods, and we had already made a run to town for Tink so you're stuck with canned food.'

There were whole canned chickens, canned bacon, canned potatoes, canned fruit and beef and vegetables and dozens and dozens and dozens of cans of fruit cocktail.

'Tink, he liked his fruit cocktail,' Cawley said, sitting on a box while he shoved other boxes under the bunk. 'I mean likes – I guess he ain't gone yet.'

John thought the wagon was nearly caved in with just his food but Cawley added the dog food. They used a

high-protein, high-fat dry dog food and he put in two hundred pounds.

'Thing is, there ain't no way you can carry everything you need. You'll need more food and so will the dogs.'

'We will?'

Cawley nodded. 'It'll go faster once you start eating it and you'll start eating it once you start working.'

'What work is there? I thought you just sat and watched the sheep.'

Cawley laughed. 'Well. That's true. And the dogs do most of the true work. But you'll be on horse for ten, twelve hours a day and that has a way of making work. Then too, things happen.'

'What do you mean – what things?'

'Things come along to happen to sheep. I don't know why it is, but if you have fifteen horses, twenty cows, and one sheep standing on a hill and a thunderstorm comes, lightning will hit the sheep. Every time. Things just happen to sheep.'

As if to emphasize his point he loaded a big box of medicine, ointments, salve, and even sutures and forceps. 'You'll know when to use them.'

That was when John had dug his heels in – halfway through the afternoon when he saw all the medicine. 'Cawley, I ain't the one for this job.'

Cawley nodded. 'Could be, could be not. But *I* ain't the one to talk to. The boss is in town, your pa, and I was just told to get you ready and take up up there.'

'I'm just fourteen and he's sending me off with six thousand head of sheep . . .'

Cawley sat back and filled his lip with chew. 'You take a shine to the old man, don't you?'

'Who do you mean?'

The old, old man – the first John. The top waddie who started all this. You're always talking about him, asking about him, wanting to know more about him.'

'Well – I guess so. Yes.'

'He stuck his kid on a drive, had him riding drag, when he was ten years old. On longhorns. Eating dust and worse for eighteen hours a day at ten. Your pa went out with the sheep to the haymeadow when he was fifteen.'

'He never talks about it.'

'He keeps close, your pa.'

John agreed. Sometimes he wanted his father to talk to him, tell him things – tell him more about his mother, his great-grandfather. Or just tell him what to do. But he was almost like Tink. Some days would go by and he wouldn't say ten or twelve words, and they might be to a horse and not all of them nice.

'Your pa summered the sheep at the haymeadow for four years, then Tink came along and he's done them ever since. So you taking them up when you're fourteen ain't so bad.' Cawley spit out the back of the wagon. 'Not bad at all. And you'll learn as you go – learn more than you'd ever believe you could.'

But now, this morning, as they were making final preparations, John stopped on the steps out of the house.

'You said yesterday that I couldn't carry everything I need to eat – for me or the dogs.'

Cawley was in back of him and he nodded. 'Yup. That's right.'

'So what happens when I run out?'

'You eat sheep.'

John turned, looking for a smile, and finally saw one. 'You're kidding . . .'

Cawley snorted. 'Time was, they ate sheep. Or cattle. Or deer and elk. But in your case one of us, me or your pa, will bring you some fodder in a month or so. You'll be fine, just fine – don't worry.'

They hooked Spud and Speck to the wagon – they settled in with no problem even with the morning coolness when they liked to pop a little – and pulled the wagon to the end of the yard by the barn – on top of everything it nearly filled the wagon to the height of the canvas top – and Cawley saddled a horse named, simply, Roan. It was a big red, almost a bloodred gelding and Cawley rode him out of the yard the half a mile to where the sheep were being held in pasture.

They were like a gray carpet – six thousand of them pushed against one end of the large holding pasture.

The wrong end, naturally, John thought. He was driving the wagon – trying to master it in the short distance from the buildings – and it was coming hard. It wasn't like riding a horse at all. He had to pull hard on the left rein to turn them left, rather than neck-reining, and had to think to turn wide on corners to make up for the length of the wagon and team.

The dogs were so excited they could barely contain themselves. All four of them had gone to the mountains with the sheep for at least three years running now. Peg was the youngest and she was four and had been doing it since she was a one-year pup.

They ran ahead of Cawley and the red gelding, came back, streaked out to the sides, ran ahead again and

couldn't stay still. At the fence they ran through the end
of the gate where there was a small gap and went out
wide around the herd at the other end of the pasture.

John loved to watch them work and was always
amazed at how smart they were.

Cawley opened the gate without getting off the red
and swung it sideways, then sat on the horse and waited.

The dogs did the rest.

Billy and Peg went out to the sides of the herd and
Jenny and Pete went up on their backs, ran across the herd
jumping from sheep to sheep and came in on the back
side of them and started them moving with barks and
small bites at some of the sheeps' legs or rear ends.

Most of the herd had done the same trip several times
and as soon as they saw the open gate and the dogs
running at them they started across the field, out the gate
and onto the road, a stream of gray backs and bleating
heads.

The dogs kept them moving, snapping and using the
small excited barks they used on stragglers and lambs
and in an hour the herd was out of the pasture.

Cawley closed the gate, grinned at John, and pointed
at the dogs. 'Ain't automation great?'

And they were on the way.

CHAPTER SIX

When the herd was moving well Cawley came back to the wagon.

'You want to ride the red and I'll take the wagon?'

John shook his head. 'It doesn't matter. What are we going to do at the highway crossing?'

'I don't know. Let's think on it.'

He spun away and let the red move up with the sheep again and John traced the path they would take in his mind.

They would stay on gravel and secondary farm roads for all of this day until just before dark. Then they hit the main highway. It wasn't a freeway, but it was well traveled with a lot of trucks and they had to cross it once they got to it because they would not be able to stop the sheep, even with the dogs' help.

When the sheep came to the road they would start to spread – they did every year – and try to go up and down the highway instead of across and it usually took one person on each side, one pushing, *and* the dogs to get across the highway. From there they stayed on gravel roads and open range for three more days, then up through the canyons to the high country on Barron land again.

With only two of them the highway was a problem and Cawley must have been thinking about it constantly because when they were four hours down the roads, moving well, the dogs keeping them compact and the pace up, Cawley came riding back.

'Any ideas?'

John shook his head. 'Just push them across and hope the dogs can hold them . . .' In truth he'd been looking at the morning, listening to the meadowlarks and feeling the warm sun on his face and thinking how pretty it looked, and felt. The sky was a clean blue – he had a shirt that looked the same color right after it was washed – and even the smell from the sheep coming back over him, the ammonia-lanolin stink of them, didn't seem bad.

He'd read a book once about a man who felt guilty because he was being paid to be a forest ranger in a national forest, doing something he loved and getting paid for it, and John thought that if the herd were cattle instead of sheep and he was riding a horse instead of the wagon he would feel the same guilt. He didn't read much, maybe two books a year other than reading for school, and the story stuck with him. Being paid for doing exactly what you wanted to do – that must be the best of all.

'Well, think on it some more,' Cawley said. 'And so will I.' He looked at the sun – he never carried a watch and went completely by the sun – and then the country around the wagon and sheep. 'We got two, two and a half hours at this place and we'll be at the highway. We want to have a plan when we get there.'

John nodded again, watched Cawley ride back up the herd and the solution came to him. Just that fast. He whistled and Cawley came back.

'I just figured it, I think. When we get closer I'll stop and take Speck out and saddle her and then help you across. When we get them lined out again I'll come back, put Speck back in, and bring the wagon up.'

Cawley seemed to think for a moment, then nodded. 'Sounds good . . . we'll do her.'

As he turned away John saw him smile and thought: He knew that. He knew to do that and he let me make the decision. But why? Why not just tell me. . . ?

It was part of all of it, he thought, part of taking the sheep up to the high country and being alone. Cawley was setting him into it a bit early, letting him be the one who made the decisions.

When they were still a half hour from the highway – John could see it two miles off, trucks and cars sliding by – he stopped the wagon, unharnessed Speck, and took his saddle out of the back of the wagon.

It took him a couple of minutes to saddle and bridle Speck and he settled into the saddle like an old friend. He would rather ride on a horse than a wagon, would rather ride a horse than walk. It was another tie to the old man. He couldn't remember when he'd started to ride. One day, when he was about eight, he was sitting on a small horse named Hammer with a saddle too big for him, riding across the short grass of the prairie with two dogs loping alongside and he had no idea how long he'd been riding or how he started.

He asked his father once and he'd just shrugged.

'I don't know. There was an old Morgan named Doofus around here and one day I came out and you were sitting on him. You were small but I can't remember how old. Three, maybe, or four. I don't know how to this day you got up on him – must have climbed a leg or something. That might have been the first time. Just seems like you was always on a horse . . .'

It didn't matter, John thought, catching up to the herd and riding out on the right to get to the highway ahead of them. He rode, that's all that mattered, and he'd rather ride than do almost anything. No. Than anything. Ride and 'see the country.' That's how the old man was told to have said it. He just '. . . rode to see the country.'

The crossing went as well as it had ever gone. He and Cawley stopped traffic from both directions and the dogs started them across.

The front end tried to spread on the highway but Peg and Billy came up to help and pushed them back, barking and biting, while John used Speck to turn back a group of twenty or so that squirted through and mixed with the stopped cars and trucks.

One car with New York plates was full of tourists and there was a girl with long brown hair who got out with a camera and John felt a little shy but tipped his hat to her. She smiled back and waved and he felt himself blushing but was glad he'd done it anyway. He sat and watched the sheep until the drag – the last of the herd – had crossed and felt her eyes on him the whole time. When they were all passed he called the dogs up – which was silly because they knew more about highway crossing than he did and were already pushing the drag down the gravel road – and turned back to where he'd left the wagon. As a little bit of show-off he let Speck jump off the road into the ditch, bound once, and jump up the other side and knew he looked good but thought it would be too much to look back and see if she was watching.

When he did turn, the car was gone and he felt stupid about doing it all. She was probably not watching anyway.

He unsaddled and harnessed Speck once more and used his tongue to make a clucking sound and move them along.

The herd was already a mile ahead and he had to catch up. Cawley would be getting hungry and the food was all in the wagon and he knew it was foolish but he looked back past the side of the wagon twice after he'd crossed the highway, thinking of the brown-haired girl.

CHAPTER SEVEN

Cawley opened a can of cold chili with a pocket knife, setting the can on one of the tires of the wagon and jacking the knife around the edge. He took a large spoon out of his shirt pocket, wiped it on his pants, and ate the chili cold in three huge bites.

John watched him and thought he must have a stomach made of cast iron. John had some canned meat and bread and made sandwiches – it was bad enough without butter or mayonnaise but at least he wasn't eating those cold bits of hardened fat he saw in Cawley's chili.

They ate in complete silence, as they usually did in the house. With Cawley and his father eating was a business to get out of the way – like putting gas in a tank on a car. Just something to get done so they could get back to whatever it was they were doing before they had to sit down to eat. And for John it was becoming that, but he still liked to chew his food slowly and think of things while he ate. The end result was that he was always the last to finish eating and the one who had to clean the table and wash the dishes, if there were any.

Cawley finished his 'lunch' in less than a minute, threw the empty chili can under the seat of the wagon, and remounted the big red.

'Pull some water for the dogs and call them in. They had some in that ditch back there but they'll need more.'

John nodded. There were two five-gallon water containers in the back and he took down a pan from the back of the wagon, filled it with water, and whistled for the dogs. They were way ahead of him, had heard the metal of the pan scraping over the bleating of the herd and were coming in four streaking black-and-white lines to the wagon. They didn't lap the water but gulped at it, biting it, and when the edge was off their thirst they were gone again – they hadn't been at the water for more than five seconds – and were back in position around the herd.

'All business, ain't they?' Cawley said, smiling. He left John and the wagon and moved back to the front of the herd. The sheep were coming to another intersection and at this one they had to turn right and would need to be guided.

John took slightly longer to finish his lunch and ate two sandwiches – one was never enough, somehow – and put things away.

As it happened Cawley did not have to go to the front after all. The dogs remembered from year to year what to do. Peg and Billy turned the front end easily enough and Jenny and Pete kept the edges of the long, gray fuzzy mass within the road and between the fences as they moved around the corner.

John never tired of watching them at work. If a sheep tried to move away from the herd, or straggled and didn't keep up, one of them – usually Jenny because she seemed to be the most watchful – would climb up on top and cross the herd at a full run, jumping from sheep to sheep to get to the one that needed personal attention. A couple of bites at the back legs, a high-pitched bark or tow or just a look, a stare, and sheep got the message. At one point John decided that maybe sheep weren't so dumb after all because they would watch the dogs and react before the dogs could get to them. A ewe would start to straggle and feel guilty about it and look for the dogs before they even came.

They made the turn easily and now it would be straight along the road for the rest of this day and the next.

John looked at his watch. It was close to four and they would stop at six for the night. Two hours would put them two or three miles and he looked ahead on the prairie as far as he thought they would get. There was a small ridge with a sinkhole full of water and he knew that was where they would spend the night, so the horses and sheep had water, because they stayed there each year when they made the drive.

'You could see all day where you were going to sleep the night.'

John had read it in one of his history books for school, a part of a journal kept by a woman crossing the plains in a wagon train in 1851, and it was true. If the country stayed flat or you were on a small rise you could see fifteen, twenty miles and that was more than the sheep could do in a day. The wagon trains didn't manage that –

barely made ten, and less if there was bad country. Some-times it might take them a week to go a mile if it was steep or there was a river to cross.

He watched Cawley and the dogs work the sheep and let Speck and Spud have their head and walk along, pulling the wagon easily on the flat ground, and wondered what it would have been like with a wagon train.

Crazy. They had to be crazy to start with just a wooden-wheeled wagon and oxen pulling it and try to get to California.

Or the original John Barron. Coming as he did with a gun and two horses.

John looked around, stood and looked back of the wagon. It would have been the same then. Almost exactly the same except there wouldn't have been fences or roads. And he'd have come riding, maybe right there, right . . . over . . . there, over that small rise, and sat on the horse and looked at the mountains in the distance and back over the prairie and north to nothing and south to nothing and he'd have said:

This is mine.

John shook is head. There were other people here. Some settlers, Indians who truly owned the land, even a couple of ranchers here and there and he'd just said it:

This is mine.

He was just four and a half years older than me, John thought. Flies had settled on the two horses and he used one of the reins to brush them off. Flies always followed the horses and sheep. Clouds of them. After a time you just got used to them, but they bit and he didn't like the horses to feel the pain.

Four and a half years older than me and he did that.
I wonder . . .

He shook his head. Stupid thinking. His father would
snort – a whoofing sound out his nose – if he knew John
was thinking that way. But the thought was there. It didn't
go away.

I wonder.

I wonder if *I* could do that if I were four and a half
years older. Just like that. Come over that rise and look
as far as I could see and say:

This is mine.

I wonder.

The time passed more quickly than John would have
thought before they came to the ridge. Maybe some of
the sheep remembered the drive to the mountains as well,
he thought, and were anxious to stop for the night.

Or it was the water. They smelled the water from the
sinkhole. The sheep hadn't had water all day and crowded
around the depression full of water.

At some time in the past the land had 'sunk' into a
shallow depression and a spring at the side of this bowl
had fed water into it. The spring was constant year-round,
seeping water, and the evaporation and water soaking into
the earth kept it from getting bigger but there was a small
pond, perhaps sixty feet across and not over two feet deep
at the most, wet year-round.

The sheep drank eagerly, fighting to get to the
water. The lambs – born three months earlier – would
take a drink, run to play, fight through the herd and take
another drink, wheel around to find a rock to play king of
the mountain on, and turn back for another drink.

John laughed, watching them, and Cawley rode up alongside the wagon.

'You laughing at the lambs?'

John nodded, 'They're full of it . . .'

'Kids, pups, and lambs – all the same. Sometimes you can watch them, lambs I mean, and they'll be standing still, looking at you and they'll just suddenly jump, straight up, hop like a grasshopper and kick. Just for fun. They're better than television . . .'

To the side of the sinkhole, just above where the spring seeped out, somebody – it might have been fifty years before – had put a small windmill and it pumped whenever the wind blew, filling a metal stock tank with fresh, pure water. Above the spring and the pond it didn't get dirty and there was a small breeze driving the windmill so that the fresh water whooshed out of the pipe in small, half-a-cup spurts.

They pulled the wagon just above the windmill and unhooked the horses and watered them and tied them out on picket ropes.

'Normally I'd hobble them – throw ankle ropes on 'em,' Cawley said. 'But they can move around a bit when they're hobbled and we might want them close in case it comes on to rain.' There was a sack of oats in the wagon and he gave each horse half a coffee can full, in old tin pans on the grass in front of them.

There was no wood – not for another fifty or so miles – so they used a small propane stove and heated up two large cans of beef stew, which they ate out of the cans. As soon as they'd finished, Cawley took out a battered coffee-pot with no insides, dumped in a handful of loose coffee grounds, and filled it with water from the end of the pipe at the stock tank.

John shook his head and drank water and wondered if he would ever come to like coffee. Cawley and his father drank it all the time, gallons of it, boiled black and thick so the grounds sank to the bottom of the pot – or some of them did. The ones that didn't they chewed on and ate.

They made it look so good that John kept trying it, but it always tasted bitter to him and made him jumpy.

It was a quiet camp and that made John think about what was happening with Tink and his father. Normally they would joke with each other – Cawley and his father were always teasing him or ragging at Tink about something – and now with just Cawley it was quiet. They set about getting ready for the night with almost no conversation.

There was a nylon tarp tied to the side of the wagon and they pulled it out to make a lean-to, pinning it to the ground with rocks.

Underneath they spread two foam pads and their sleeping bags. It had been a hot day but the nights became cold and the bags would be welcome.

When the beds were down Cawley brought a braided horsehair rope from his saddle and spread it around the bed area.

'For snakes,' he said. 'Keeps them out of your bag.'

John had heard of it of course. Rattlesnakes were supposed not to crawl over horsehair and he knew many cowboys who believed in it.

But he'd been to an exhibit in Cheyenne once where they had a pit of snakes and they had a horsehair rope in the pit and the rattlers crawled all over it.

Besides, if he saw one snake a year it was unusual. There just weren't that many and with all the sheep and the dogs he didn't think they'd be running to get in his bag with him. But he didn't say anything.

With the beds ready John took down the same large pan they'd used to water the dogs and filled it with dry dog food and set it by the tailgate. The dogs would come in to sleep and eat as they wished, then head out to watch the sheep again.

Cawley rummaged around in the back of the wagon – it was so full, he had to crawl on his stomach up on top of the load – and came out with a small kerosene lantern.

He lit the lantern and hung it from a nail beneath the wagon box. It cast a yellow light about ten feet and they crawled into their sleeping bags still in silence.

Cawley filled his lip with snuff, spit once to the side, and lay back. John had wadded his jacket into a pillow and had a metal button in his cheek. He wiggled it around, settled back and closed his eyes.

'You got any questions?' Cawley asked.

'About what?'

'About what to do with the sheep when you get up to the high country. You seem a little fussed up about it and I thought you might have some questions.'

John rolled onto his back. Cawley had blown the lantern out and there was no moon so it was pitch-dark. A million, he thought – I must have a million of them. And that was the trouble. There were so many he didn't know where to start, what to ask.

'No,' he said, finally, 'I can't think of one.'

'Well that's good then,' Cawley said, spitting again. 'Your pa wanted me to teach you some of this on the way and if you know it all it makes my job easier.'

John didn't say anything.

'That was slick, how you tipped your hat to that girl at the highway crossing.'

Cawley, John thought, never missed a thing. He felt his cheeks burn in the dark, was glad Cawley couldn't see them.

'She appreciate it?'

John had to laugh, remembering. 'No, I don't think so. She just drove off.'

'Well, that happens, don't it?'

'Yes, I guess it does.'

'Is your heart broke?'

'No.'

'Good night.'

'Good night.' John closed his eyes and tried to sleep but his thoughts mixed so that he thought of the girl in the car and his father and Tink and his great-grandfather all at once until, finally, they all swirled together and he slept.

CHAPTER EIGHT

The sheep did not want to leave the water in the morning. The dogs and Cawley would get the front end moving and the rest of the herd would just stand and watch them leave and the ones that started would try to circle around the dogs and get back.

John sat on the wagon seat and watched for a time, then unhooked Speck and saddled her and helped by riding back and forth across the rear of the herd yelling and popping a piece of rope he'd taken from the wagon until they were moving.

It was slow at first, and the dogs had to work overtime to get the herd moving and keep them moving. They ran back and forth over the herd, yipping in high, excited barks and biting, pushing, always pushing. At one point John laughed when he looked around and saw Peg standing on the back of a large ewe spitting bits of wool out of her mouth.

At last they were moving and through that day there

were no highway crossings to plague them so that things ran smoothly. Speck and Spud had long before figured out what was happening and John didn't have to steer or even talk to them. They walked down the middle of the small, rutted road that led west toward the mountains and John leaned back in the seat and enjoyed the ride. Twice he caught himself dozing, the warm sun pushing him down into the seat, and after they had moved the herd past a small side road – a driveway into a pasture – Cawley came back. He tied the red to the tailgate of the wagon and climbed up beside John.

'I thought of some things,' he said.

'What things?'

'About the sheep and the dogs. Things you might want to know.'

John sat up. Cawley filled his lip with snuff and spit. 'The problem is that I'm going to have to turn around and head back as soon as we get there. There's the ranch to take care of while your pa is with Tink. So I won't be able to stay with you and get you started. You're going to be on your own just about twenty minutes after we get there.'

John nodded. 'I figured that.'

'So we can talk while we ride. Look, looky there. . . .' He pointed to where a rebellious ewe had gone off the road and about thirty sheep followed her, lambs jumping and leaping over the older sheep. Jenny and Pete peeled off from the right side of the herd and turned the small band and headed them back into the main body.

'Ain't it fun – just to watch them work?'

John nodded.

'They got something,' Cawley said. 'With the sheep I

mean. They got something in their heads and the sheep understand it and know they know about sheep. I've puzzled on it some but I guess it must go way back.'

With the strays back in Jenny and Pete settled once more into the positions they had held, although Jenny now and then would stop and stand on her hind legs and look to the rear of the herd to make certain all the sheep were coming.

'Like that – she was never taught that. They were never taught nothing, really. Just born into them. And the other dogs don't do that, stand like that and check the rear.' He laughed. 'They would, you know, if she didn't. But they figure since she's doing it they don't have to so they don't. They figure on it, figure on it and work it out.'

'Like when they look at you,' John said.

Cawley nodded. 'That's it, exactly.'

Sometimes the dogs – usually one dog at a time – would come and sit down in front of a person and look into his eyes for a full half a minute, just look and be thinking of something, trying to see something. The first time it happened it spooked John. But after a time he thought they might just be saying hi, or that they loved him. It was a soft look. And he always reached out and petted them and saw that Cawley and Tink and his father did the same. And then the dog would walk away and sit or lie down and maybe a half hour or an hour later he would come back and do the same thing.

'They know things,' Cawley said again, shaking his head. 'They know more things than there are to know under the sun. . . .'

The two rode in silence for a little time and John

thought on how he didn't really know anything about Cawley at all. Not where he came from nor if he'd ever been married nor how he'd lived before he came to work at the ranch or if he had just been there mostly forever and then he thought he didn't know any of that about Tink, either. He could ask, he knew, but the words didn't come and he thought that was like his father, to not talk, not ask. And maybe like the old man.

'You got to take care of them,' Cawley said suddenly, his voice startling John. 'They're smart but they're dumb too. They'll do too much for you because of how they feel about you. Dogs don't think of the end, only the beginning. So you've got to take care of them.'

'How do you mean?'

'Well, like food and water. If you don't water them and feed them they'll keep going and keep going and then just drop. You've got to keep them supplied all the time.'

'Like horses.'

'Same as.' Cawley nodded. 'Same as. Except horses won't go past a point unless you drive 'em, which of course ain't right. But dogs will. They'll keep on going until it kills them, even if you ain't pushing them. So you get up in that camp, you keep a pan of food and water by the wagon. They'll drink out of a stream, too, but you keep water handy for them all the same.'

John nodded and they went back to silence.

The land changed rapidly now. Even at the slow pace the sheep moved. They were climbing – Speck and Spud had to pull harder on the wagon and their breathing picked up as they worked – and the country was altered as if a line had been drawn and they had crossed the line.

Instead of flat prairie they were in the low, rolling hills that led into the mountains and where there had been no trees – not just few, but *no* trees – there were now scrub pines and aspens showing, standing in small patches. The road had dwindled as well while he and Cawley were talking. For a time the day before and earlier in the morning they had been on gravel roads but they had narrowed and finally disappeared into twin shallow ruts the horses followed.

The fences were gone as well and the dogs worked frantically to keep the sheep in one herd and moving. Without fences to hold them along the road they kept trying to spread out and they would sometimes actually run from the main herd and try to hide in the small stands of short trees.

The dogs kept bringing them back, circling out and driving them back into the herd and John was once more amazed at their endurance. During the hot part of the afternoon, when the horses slowed and the sun seemed to crush everything into the ground, the dogs worked tirelessly, their tongues hanging down half a foot, slobbering while they ran, running back to the wagon to get water out of a pan John would put on the ground for them and then back to the herd.

Cawley left the wagon to help, running the big red back and forth across the rear of the herd to try to give the dogs a break and between the four dogs and Cawley they kept the herd moving.

John felt frustrated. On the two drives he'd done he was on a horse, helping push them, and to sit on a wagon and watch Cawley grated on him. But he did it quietly and finally, toward evening, they came into a clearing where they usually spent the second night and Cawley called the dogs in and they let the herd spread.

They set up a rough camp, again heating cans of food on a stove and eating out of the cans. Cawley said nothing until they were done eating and he had brewed coffee, then he leaned back and belched.

'We'll make the meadow tomorrow.'

Which is what somebody said every year but John nodded. 'By noon.'

'Is it me or are they getting more stubborn?' Cawley said. 'The sheep, I mean.'

'They seemed rough to push today – I wouldn't know, though, sitting on my butt on the wagon all day.'

Cawley nodded. 'I figured that would twist your tail a bit. But it's your wagon, ain't it? You're going to live in it so you take care of it.'

Cawley lay back and was asleep instantly, his breath coming low and raspy, but John sat awake with his feet down in his bag for over an hour thinking on what Cawley had said.

He was going to live in the wagon.

For three months.

Alone.

Well. There were the dogs. And the sheep. And the mountains.

Before he went to sleep the last thought in his head was strangely about the girl in the car again. She had looked right at him, into his eyes, when he'd tipped his hat – just straight, blue eyes.

And he'd never see her again.

CHAPTER NINE

John was wrong.

They did not get to the haymeadow the next day at noon. It was closer to seven, almost dark, when they finally pulled into the west end of the meadow.

It was more than a meadow. More than just hay. It was a wide, shallow valley between two rows of peaks. The haymeadow itself was four sections, but the whole valley was close to four miles across and nearly eight miles long and so beautiful, John thought, that it almost took his breath away.

And it was a complete surprise. In the middle a stream moved down through the whole length of the canyon. It ran nearly straight and here and there a stand of aspens grew along the edge. The stream left the valley through a narrow cut between two hills – small mountains, really – and then worked its way down into the prairies ten and more miles below.

It was impossible to see the valley, to know that it was

there until passing through the cut between the hills and it must have been a shock the first time the old man had seen it.

It was a perfect summer pasture. The evening cool kept the flies from being a problem for the stock, and the water and daylight sun kept the grass growing so that it came to John's knees when he walked.

'Something, ain't it?' Cawley said as they followed the sheep through the entry between the hills. 'Sure wished I owned it. . . .'

We did, John thought. The Barrons did own it. And lost it.

Most of the sheep knew where they were, knew that the drive was done, and they spread out and started to eat.

'Got to push them a bit more,' Cawley said, popping his rope at the rear of the herd. 'Get these ones in the rear up into the good grass and near water. If they don't get to water some of them won't make it.'

They had come all day without water and John knew that sheep had a way of dying with little or no reason.

The dogs also knew where they were but sensed Cawley's urgency and ripped into the trailing end of the herd with a vengeance, snapping and barking and spitting wool until all of them, even the lambs, were up in good grass and had easy access to the stream.

Every year they pulled the wagon approximately up to the center of the valley where a small patch of aspens provided a windbreak and some shade. It was where Tink liked to be and John decided he might as well do the same.

It took him almost an hour more to get there and by then it was totally dark. Cawley lighted the lantern and hung it from the wagon and they began to unload in the dark. The wagon had a small set of stairs – two steps – and the third time Cawley hung a foot in a step and tripped coming down in the dark he swore and they decided to wait until daylight to finish setting up the camp.

'Before I break my neck,' he said.

So they made the bedrolls and tarp ready, set up dog food and water, heated up two cans of stew and ate and went to bed and asleep without saying ten more words.

There was something, John thought just before sleep took him – something about the valley that kept you from saying much and made you talk quietly when you did talk.

John opened his eyes.

The smell of coffee made his mouth water. He hated coffee but loved the smell of it brewing and he sat up to see Cawley up, dressed and with a fire going.

'I've got to bust out,' Cawley said. 'I can make it in a long day and a short one if I keep moving. I thought you needed sleep so I let you be. You did some rambling about that girl in the car and I thought maybe you wanted to dream a little more. . . .'

'I did not.'

Cawley smiled. 'Well, you don't really know, do you?'

He rolled his bedroll into a tube and tied it, stood. In the background John saw that the big red was already saddled and waiting patiently.

Cawley stopped, looked once more down at John. 'Any questions?'

'I . . .'

He was going to say a hundred things. I don't know

anything. I don't think I can do this. I can't, I can't ... it isn't fair to leave me here alone. I don't know what I'm doing – and in the end that's what came out. 'I don't know what I'm doing.'

Cawley laughed. 'Well, hell, none of us do, do we?'

'But I mean it. It's not a joke. I'll try this 'cause Pa said to try it but I don't, Cawley – I don't know what to do.'

Cawley nodded. 'I understand – but the dogs and sheep will tell you how it's done. You know what they used to say, back when the old man was running the spread?'

John shook his head.

'Keep a horse to hand.'

He turned and walked to the red, tied his bedroll across in back of the saddle, swung up and mounted, and set off at a pacing walk without looking back or waving or saying another word.

And John sat in his sleeping bag and watched him leave, watched him ride until he was a small dot at the end of the valley, a dot that disappeared in the cut between the hills. John watched even when he was gone, watched the place between the hills and found himself wishing, hoping, praying that everything would reverse and a dot would reappear and grow larger and it would be Cawley coming back to tell him it was a joke.

But it did not. The dot stayed gone and John flopped back in the bag and looked up at the underside of the tarp.

I am the only person in the valley, he thought, and then he said it aloud. 'I am the only person here.'

It just didn't seem possible that his pa would drop him up here with six thousand sheep for the summer. Not like this. Not alone.

He started to feel sorry for himself, then remembered the old man. Four, five years older than John and he claimed the whole place – alone.

John pulled his boots on and rolled his bedroll. It was high morning and he had a lot of work to do – unload the wagon, get camp squared away, get settled for the first night alone with the herd.

But the coffee on the fire still smelled good. He stopped work for a moment and poured some in the tin cup he'd used for drinking water and took a sip, hoping that he would like it. It tasted bitter and he spit it out and turned back to the bedroll.

Just as he finished rolling the bedroll and was reaching for the tie cord to tie it he heard one of the dogs barking and the bleating of sheep and over it all the high-pitched rattle of a snake, almost a buzz-hissing sound.

He dropped everything and ran for the horses.

CHAPTER TEN

They weren't there.

The night before, he'd turned them loose so they could graze and shake and roll. Cawley hadn't said anything so he hadn't retied them. They would stay around the sheep herd, or nearby, and Speck always came when he called.

Except they weren't nearby. They were over a quarter mile up the valley, along the river. He could see them and he yelled for Speck. She raised her head, looked at him, and started walking toward him and Spud followed. But she wasn't hurrying, stopping to take a bite of the fresh green grass next to the stream now and then, and she would be fifteen minutes getting to him.

He looked the other way, to the herd, and saw that on the side along the creek there was a cleared area – a round spot in the middle of the gray backs. Peg was there, dancing around something on the ground, bouncing on her front feet, getting close to it and away. He saw Billy coming across the herd from the far side to help her.

John looked back to Speck. Too far. He started running toward the herd.

Keep a horse to hand, he thought – each step pounding it into him. A horse to hand, a horse to hand, a horse to hand . . .

It was probably not three hundred yards to run but the altitude caught him. They had climbed for two days and were close to nine thousand feet – up from six thousand or so. In fifty yards he was winded and could not run faster.

He did not see the snake until he was thirty or forty paces away.

It wasn't huge – perhaps two or two and a half feet. It was past coiling and raised in the powerful S shape they used just before striking, the S up and back so that only a third of the snake was on the ground and the rest of it was in the air and free to strike.

'Peg, back – get back!' The snake struck at her but she was dancing backward as it flew out and the snake missed by almost nothing. A tiny gap.

He caught Peg's collar and held her back and when she realized he was holding her she sat quietly and watched the snake.

Billy had come by this time and was circling warily, his nose almost to the ground, well out and away from the snake.

All right, John thought. It's controlled. It's all controlled.

With all the activity around it calmed a bit, the snake lowered itself into a coil again, the rattles – John counted ten – buzzing now and then in short spurts as Billy moved or it sensed John.

'Anybody hit?' John asked. Peg seemed to be fine and Billy was holding well back.

He'd have to kill the snake. He didn't particularly want to – not like most people out here, he thought. Some would drive five miles extra to run over one. He had always thought that if they left him alone he'd leave them alone and he almost liked their attitude.

But that was just it – the snake wouldn't leave them alone. It was where the sheep had to pasture and if he didn't kill it they'd run into it again and again.

He picked up a large rock from the streambed, so heavy he had to lift it over his head with both hands, and brought it down on the snake as hard and as fast as he could.

There were several more buzzes as the snake's nerves wiggled the tail but it was dead and he turned to go back to the wagon.

Billy came in close and smelled the snake, jumped back when the tail wiggled, then went back to the herd. Pete and Jenny were working together and had never left their positions on the far edge of the sheep.

Peggy watched John walk away, sitting still.

'What?' He turned. She was still sitting there, watching him, not moving to get back to the sheep.

'What's the matter now?'

Then he saw the lamb.

The sheep had cleared a circle around the snake – thirty, forty feet across. They had gone back to grazing almost immediately, heads down, many not even watching as John killed the snake.

Directly across the cleared area from John a lamb was biting at its side, chewing at the wool and drooling.

'Oh, no . . .'

Peg had known. The lamb was hit. It must have come on the snake first and been struck in the side and Peg was waiting for him to do something.

He ran across the clear area. The sheep jumped at the sudden movement and ran away a short distance – all except the lamb and its mother. She stayed near him, making worried bleating sounds as the lamb twisted in short circles trying to reach its side.

John caught it by wool on the back and held it to the ground with his knee. It struggled for a moment, then lay still.

'Where is it? Where . . .' The wool was half an inch thick and very tight and he thought for a moment that he wouldn't be able to find it or that the snake hadn't been able to get through the wool.

He dug with his fingers, pushing the wool sideways – it was wet with spit where the lamb had been chewing – and finally he saw where the snake had hit.

Low on the side, just in back of the shoulder there were two small wounds, slightly swollen, one a little bigger than the other.

What did he do?

What could he do?

In school in biology they'd had a full day on snakes and how they bit, what the venom did, and he somehow couldn't remember any of it.

The lamb struggled against his hands and the mother came in to lean down and smell it. She looked up at John with frightened eyes.

She can't know, John thought. 'It ain't good. . . .' he

said aloud, then realized he was talking to sheep.

Tink, he thought – he must have talked to the sheep all the time. What would Tink do? What would his pa or Cawley do? What would the old man have done?

And he knew.

They would shoot the lamb.

All of them would shoot the lamb.

CHAPTER ELEVEN

'No,' he said. 'I don't think they're right. . . .'

He stood and picked the lamb up. It did not want to come and fought against his hold, bleating. Peg came running back, brought by the disturbance, and tried to herd the mother – who was following John and bleating anxiously at the lamb – back to the herd.

'Peg, leave it be – she can come.'

The dog stopped, caught by the tone in his voice more than any command, and John pointed with his chin because his arms were holding the lamb. 'Back – herd. Get 'em.'

She knew that, knew the command to 'get 'em,' and she turned back to the main part of the herd, pushing them farther and farther away from the dead snake.

'We're going to try to help him,' he said – and realized once more that he was talking to a sheep. Well, why not. 'We'll try. . . .'

At the trailer he tied the lamb to a wheel with the end

of the rope that held the tarp and rummaged in the boxes inside until he found the box of medicines for the sheep.

Mostly it was salve – Corona. Balm to put on scrapes and minor wounds. And cans of pine tar to put on cuts to keep the flies off. There was nothing for snakebites.

'I'll have to cut it.' He remembered from biology that there was some argument over whether or not to cut and suck a snakebite wound. Some said it helped, others said it didn't, and in either case it was dangerous because taking the venom in your mouth could be bad if there was a small cut or cavity. But if he cut it – he couldn't bring himself to suck the wound – it might help, might allow some of the venom to drain.

He took the folding knife out of the case on his belt. In the box there were several bottles of disinfectant and he poured some strong-smelling purple fluid from one of the bottles onto his knife blade. He'd seen his father do the same before digging a staple out of a horse's hoof.

He held the lamb down with his knee, pushed the wool away from the bite mark with his finger, and pushed with the knife.

A tiny hole appeared and the lamb blatted and the mother came closer, looking down on the lamb and John.

It wasn't enough.

He'd have to cut it really deep. Across both fang marks and then down vertically across each of them in turn – that's what they'd said in biology. The teacher – Mr Fender. It's always so neat in a classroom, John thought suddenly. This and that, just so. A wound. You cut or you didn't cut. But here – the side of a sheep that's kicking all the time, wool all over the wound, dirt, flies.

He took a breath, held it, and slashed across the two bites, then down vertically across each of them.

The lamb kicked and bucked sideways, lunging up against his knee and blood welled instantly into the wool, dripping on the ground and against John's leg where it pushed the lamb down.

So much blood.

It seemed to be endless and he wondered if he'd cut an artery by accident but didn't think there would be an artery running down the side of the lamb and then realized that he hadn't the slightest idea of where a lamb's arteries *did* run.

He stood back and away, the knife hanging at his side, and the lamb jumped up, twisted, and tried to bite at its side again.

In a moment the blood seemed to lessen and not long after that, while he was watching, it slowed to a stop.

Pine tar, he thought. They always put pine tar on cuts to keep the flies out. But if the pine tar was there, would the venom still come out? His father told him that back in the old days, before they used rubber bands to castrate the lambs, they used a knife and they would dab pine tar on the wound to keep the flies out.

He dug through the medicine box and found the pine tar – a can with a Pop Top. He probed at the lid with his knife and it finally came open.

Inside was a thick black tar. He used a stick to remove a clump and smeared it on the side of the lamb, getting some in his hair and on his face and clothes as he worked.

When he was done he threw the stick aside and stood and looked down on the lamb. It was on its feet, goobered in tar – during the struggle much of the tar had gone astray and there were dark marks all along the side of the lamb.

'There.'

All of this had taken twenty or thirty minutes – it was, he thought, maybe forty minutes altogether since he got up – and he looked at the morning sun, just coming into the cut between the two hills at the entrance to the canyon, and wished he hadn't come.

I could've said no, he thought. I could have. But he knew he couldn't. Saying no just didn't come into it. His father would not have sent him up here if he hadn't thought John could do it. And then there was the old man – the old, old man. He would have done it, and more.

First morning, first hour, and look at it, he thought – I've got one lamb hurt, a mess, and I haven't even unpacked the trailer.

He turned to start unpacking but as his eyes moved off the lamb it went down – as if hit with a hammer. It lay on its side, raising and lowering its head in jerky movements.

John kneeled next to it again but there was nothing he could do.

The lamb's legs and feet made running motions, it bleated low – the ewe came forward and smelled the wound on the lamb's side, snorted – and the lamb curved up at each end, obviously in great pain, and then it died.

It was very fast. Half a breath came in, went out, and the lamb was gone.

The ewe nudged it, pushed at it, tried to get it up and then stood next to it, guarding it.

'Ahh . . .' John rubbed the back of his neck. 'Ahh, hell.'

He picked the lamb up and waded across the stream away from the camp, the ewe following. There was a thick stand of willows and he went inside them, found some rocks and laid the lamb down and made a small pile of rocks over it.

He did not know why he did this. He had seen many lambs die. During lambing when they came fast sometimes eight or ten would die almost at once and they had a pile of dead sheep and lambs in back of the lambing pens every spring that Cawley used the tractor to load and haul out to a gulley for the coyotes and buzzards to clean up.

But this was different.

This, he thought, was his lamb – a lamb he had been supposed to care for – and it had died and needed to be covered.

The ewe had followed him into the willows and he pushed her away from the rocks that covered the body, tried to get her to go back to the herd. But she wouldn't leave. She kept working back around him to get to the rocks, smelling the dead lamb through them.

Finally he left her there but he kept looking back at her, standing over the small pile of rocks, until the willows covered her and he couldn't see her and then he thought of her. He stood, wondering what to do next and thought he should unpack the trailer but he kept thinking of the ewe and it bothered him so that he went back across the stream to check on her. She was still there, standing with her head down, her nose smelling the rocks that covered the lamb. She looked up at him and bleated when he walked up to her.

'Yeah – I know. I feel bad too – but you have to leave it now.' He tried to push her away again but once more she evaded him and at last he decided to let nature take its course. Short of dragging her away and tying her to a tree he didn't see how to stop her.

At the camp he reached into the wagon to pull out the first box and there was a sudden high-pitched barking from the direction of the herd. He turned to see Billy on the far side of the sheep, dancing around something on the ground and he thought, oh, great, another snake, and he turned to see if Speck was handy but she was away and gone back up the canyon a quarter mile or more so he turned and started to run.

Keep, he thought, his breath coming in cutting rasps – *keep* a horse to hand.

CHAPTER TWELVE

It was not a snake.

He could tell well before he arrived at the clearing, his breath tearing at his lungs, his legs wobbly – he could tell by the smell.

It was a skunk.

The sheep had wandered on a skunk or it had come upon them. How it happened didn't matter. What mattered was that it was a skunk and that Billy was close to it.

The sheep had moved away except for one ewe that kept rubbing her face on the ground and snorting to clear her nose out. In the middle of the cleared space – almost the same size as the snake had caused – stood a skunk on all fours, its tail raised but not fully ready to spray. Billy stood with his shoulder hair up, his tail plumed and his teeth bared. The stink was everywhere.

When the dog saw John coming he took it as encouragement. He feinted once to the left and then dodged right and tore into the skunk.

'Billy!'

The reaction was immediate. The skunk instantly raised further until its back legs were off the ground, pulled its tail up over the top, and caught Billy head-on with a vaporous cloud.

The stink drove John back but it didn't slow Billy down even momentarily. Caught square in the face, half blinded, he continued his attack and snatched the skunk up, shaking him so that John could hear the bones crunch.

'Billy – drop it!'

And he did, finally, drop the skunk. But not until it had sprayed itself empty and not until it was broken and dead and by that time Billy was drenched and running in circles rubbing his head and face on the ground to clear his eyes and get rid of the stink.

'Oh . . .' John had been too close and caught the edge of the spray and it was in his clothes.

He found a stick and hooked the dead skunk and dragged it down the canyon away from the sheep – though they had moved well away from the smell on their own.

Then he came back to Billy.

'We've got to get some of that off you. Come on.'

Billy hung back but at length followed and John led him down to the stream and walked in, fully clothed.

'Come on – *now.*'

Billy's tail went down but he came until he was standing in the belly-deep water next to John and he continued to stand quietly while John used his hands to cup water and tried to wash the stink out of him.

It didn't work very well and soon the smell seemed to be smeared all over the dog, all over John, all over the world.

At last he gave up and let Billy go back to the herd. The dog shook the water off and rubbed in the dirt some more, then went to work on the far side of the herd and John looked down to see that he was completely soaked, smelled worse than before, and somehow – spitting and gagging – he had apparently gotten it inside his mouth.

Everything, he thought, for the rest of my life will taste like this – forever. He let his eyes find the sun – not two hours had passed since the snake had hit the lamb.

The first day wasn't half over, not even started, and he was a mess and just when he wondered what could happen to make it worse he heard a short yip-yip of pain and looked up at the herd to see Pete running on three legs around the back side of the herd, headed toward the wagon.

John ran from the stream toward the wagon and arrived – soaking wet, stinking, his hat gone somewhere – just after Pete.

He knelt next to the dog, raised the right leg, and the dog screamed. Not the leg, he thought, lower – the foot.

He turned the pad back up carefully and stopped. Half the pad on one of the toes was torn almost completely away, hung by a shred of skin. He must have stepped on a broken shard of rock or flint, something very sharp. The dog squirmed and whined in pain when the flap of skin and flesh wiggled and John fought a rising sick feeling in the middle of his stomach. The dogs, he thought – the dogs were everything. He couldn't do this without the dogs. He might not be able to do it anyway, but without the dogs he didn't stand a chance and now Pete was crippled. Just like that. Torn like that.

What could he do?

He had to help Pete. Somehow fix the foot and help him but it was so bad – the damage looked so awful. How could he get the flap back in place and hold it?

He tied Pete to the same twine he'd tied the lamb to, then dug around again in the medicine box. There were liniments and salve and some bandages and an elastic kind of covering bandage called Vet-Wrap. There were also some bottles of a blue-colored disinfectant.

So.

He brought a cup of water from the stream and washed the wound. Then he raised the bottle and poured some of the blue medicine into the cut.

Pete screamed and jerked and snapped at the bottle.

'Sorry, sorry.' John spoke in a low voice, tried to sound confident – which was more than he felt.

He took a gauze pad from a small container in the box and put it on the torn pad, then wrapped the whole thing with the Vet-Wrap, which had a stickiness to it that held it in place. When it was done he leaned back and looked and almost smiled.

On the end of Pete's leg there was a large pink balloon – the Vet-Wrap was pink – that made it look like he'd stepped in six or seven pounds of sticky bubble gum. Pete stood with a forlorn look on his face, the foot raised.

'Well – maybe it'll work.' John rubbed the dog's ears and turned to himself.

He still smelled like the bad end of a skunk and was soaked.

'So I'll do my laundry,' he said to Pete.

He stripped to the skin, emptied his pockets – a billfold

with nothing but some pictures, one of his mother, one of his father, and three dollars, a pocketknife, and a fingernail clipper. He hated long fingernails.

With his clothes emptied and the belt stripped out he walked naked into the stream, sat down and washed them and himself without soap as best as he could. Then he hung the clothes on nearby willows to dry, found his other shirt and jeans in the wagon and started to put them on.

He was just jamming the second leg into the stiff jeans when his thinking was stopped, and almost his heart, by a high-pitched scream. He knew the sound, had heard it before – it was either a bobcat or mountain lion, he couldn't tell which. But it didn't matter. It came from up the side of the canyon, above the sheep, and he looked up to see roughly six thousand sheep coming straight at him at a dead run.

But there's no room, he thought – not for all of you to be in camp. We just don't have the room . . .

And they were over him. He stood and braced his legs and they tried to go around him. But they were panicking and wide-eyed, snorting snot, bleating, and many of them ran in to him and he knew he could never stand. He'd never heard of anybody being killed in a sheep stampede but he didn't want to try to be the first.

He saw that Pete had run under the wagon and he made a dive for the small space, bounced off woolly backs, went down, staggered back up and scrambled in next to Pete, around in back of the wheel while the sheep ran over and around everything else.

'My clothes . . .'

When the mass of running sheep hit the willows they went down and John's clothes went with them, churned into the ground by thousands of feet.

In less than a minute it was finished. All the sheep and lambs had crossed the stream and the front of the herd was grazing peacefully on the opposite side of the canyon from the scream.

There was no second scream. John crawled out from under the wagon. It was probably a bobcat – the lions were usually higher – and if so there was little danger. Lions killed sheep but the smaller bobcats would only take lambs when they were very small and alone. They almost never bothered adult sheep or protected lambs. It was probably just marking its territory.

But the damage was done.

The camp was a shambles – or actually, he thought, it looked very neat. Almost swept. The box of medicines had been tipped and everything scattered and driven into the dirt. The steps were carried off the wagon and broken apart, the boards thrown every which way. He found his shirt and pants after some searching and almost threw the shirt away. The pants, being heavier material, had come through with just a few small cuts. The shirt was of thinner cloth and was literally in shreds. But he had brought only three work shirts for the whole summer, and one lined jacket, three pairs of pants, so he decided to keep the shirt. For rags, if nothing else.

His saddle had been on the ground next to the wagon and it had been tossed sideways but he'd always kept it oiled and pliable and the leather was tough. It had not been hurt.

The wagon had remained upright and everything inside it was all right.

'It could be worse,' he said, and looked around to see that Pete had torn the bandages off his foot, had chewed through the twine holding him to the wagon, and was limping back to the herd to help the other three dogs.

'Pete – come here!'

The dog stopped, looked at John, wagged his tail, looked at the sheep, then back at John once more, then back to the sheep and he limped again toward the herd.

And John couldn't stop him.

He stood, holding his rags, the camp in a shambles and he couldn't stop the dog and realized he had no control.

Over anything.

CHAPTER THIRTEEN

The day passed, somehow, with nothing truly getting done.

He found some saddle oil in a box in the trailer and cleaned and oiled his saddle and put it under the wagon. Then he started to unload and rearrange the inside of the wagon so that he could sleep there for the night and he found a needle and thread and he tried to patch his shirt and pants and in some way the whole day went that way. One thing to another until it was dark and he really couldn't see that anything was done. Even the wagon wasn't squared away. The bunk was clear, but the rest of it was still a shambles and when dark came he lighted the lantern, hung it from the bow holding the canvas up, and sat in the yellow glow and ate a can of cold beef stew with a metal spoon. He caught himself starting to wipe the spoon on his pants leg, smiled, and went outside and washed it in the stream, using sand to clean it and rinsing it when it was spotless.

He went to bed not so much because he was tired as to get away from the day, his first day, and he was nearly asleep when he remembered he hadn't put down dog food. He climbed out barefoot and put a pan down, kicking himself mentally for being so stupid. All four of the dogs were there to eat, sitting watching him, waiting for the food, and he relighted the lantern and used the light to examine Pete's foot.

The pad had already worked back into place and seemed to be sticking there, healing in. It was impossible, but it was there. He touched it and Pete jerked his paw away, went back to eating, and when he was done he returned to the herd at a run. He still limped, but he was moving better and John went back to sleep wondering how it could begin to heal that fast.

The first smash of thunder awakened him, seemed to come from inside his mind. It was close, so close he could smell the stink of burned air and he was sitting up, awake, before he realized what had done it.

He knew mountain thunder was worst – because you were right inside it, right in the clouds. And he'd heard it before. But it still surprised him, to be in the middle of a storm.

Lightning came fast for seven or eight minutes, seemed to smack back and forth across the valley, from peak to peak and into the trees and was followed instantly and almost continuously by the thunder and made it so bright he could almost have read.

And loud. It actually *thunders*, he thought, jumping for the end of the wagon and opening the door to watch.

He could see the sheep in the constant blue light and they were afraid – were milling and bleating, though he couldn't hear them well. The dogs were working the edges of the herd restlessly except for Jenny.

He couldn't find Jenny.

'Jenny!' He called her name several times but she was nowhere near the herd – only three dogs were there.

Then she showed.

She was under the wagon and came out slowly, her tail down, her ears laid back.

'Jenny – what's the matter?'

She was terrified of the thunder, stiff with fear.

'Well – it is scary, isn't it?' It was starting to rain and she looked so bedraggled, so afraid and lonely that he smiled.

'Why don't you come on in?'

He motioned with his hand and she was inside the trailer in part of a second, almost knocking him down.

She jumped on the cot, curled up about halfway up from the bottom, and tucked her nose under her tail.

'I see,' he said. 'You must have done this with Tink.' He smiled. 'Well, I guess it's all right . . .'

John slid inside the bag, scrunching his legs past the sleeping dog, and blew the lantern out by raising the globe and blowing across the top. But the light from the lightning kept a dim blue glow going inside the trailer for a long time and just when it seemed to be stopping, the lightning cutting back, the rain started.

It was not hard at first, but grew in intensity until it drummed on the waterproof tarp so that he could not hear himself think. He sat up, lighted the lantern, but everything – for a change – seemed to be all right. The tarp was not leaking except for a small drip around the chimney hole but that was nothing. Even as he watched, the yellow light making shadows jump, the rain and noise let off and the storm moved off up the canyon, back up into the mountains.

Where it belongs, John thought, blowing the lantern out again and lying back in the bed.

He closed his eyes and waited for sleep but it didn't come. Something was working at him, bothering him, and he couldn't pin it down. Something about the storm.

He waited, letting his mind wander, but nothing came and, finally, his eyes closed and he went to sleep with his hand on Jenny's forehead.

CHAPTER FOURTEEN

John's eyes were open and he was sitting up but he couldn't think why he was awake.

It was pitch-dark and totally silent. Even the sheep were quiet, down for the night. John found his digital watch and pushed the illuminating button.

Three in the morning.

No sound, not even night sounds. Jenny had been asleep and when he raised up she did the same, raised her head and looked at him.

'The storm is over,' he said. Way off, now that he was awake, miles away in the mountains he heard faint rumbling. 'Why am I awake?'

Jenny moved from the bed, stretched, and went to the door of the trailer.

'Back to work, eh?' He dropped his feet to the floor and padded to the small door, let her out, and stood for a moment on the steps, listening, waiting.

For what?

There was nothing wrong. Overhead the sky was brilliantly clear. While there was no moon the stars splashed across the sky and gave enough light so that he could see the sheep, bedded, sleeping, or watching him. Jenny trotted off silently to the edge of the herd and sat, watching.

Waiting.

For what? It was there, something was there but he couldn't for the life of him think of anything wrong, anything that needed doing.

He shook his head, shrugged, and returned to the trailer. The night was cold – he had seen his breath when he was standing on the steps – and his sleeping bag was still warm. He zipped it up to his shoulder and lay, still awake, thinking.

Something.

Something bothered him. Was it the sheep? The dogs? No . . . it was all right. Everything was all right.

It was just the day, he finally decided. It had been a rough first day and the hangover from it was bothering him. Maybe tomorrow would be better and he could settle in . . .

He closed his eyes and sleep started to come and just there, just between being awake and being asleep – he almost thought he was dreaming it – he heard a faint sound.

Nearly thunder.

Maybe that was it. It was so warm in the bag and he was so sleepy and the sound was so faint he thought it was more of the storm up in the mountains, the far-off rumbling of clouds bumping in the peaks. What had his father said that time?

Oh, yeah, the devil bowling. The thunder was the devil bowling up in the mountains. It was something his grandfather had said and before him, his great-grandfather. The thunder was the devil bowling up in the peaks but there was something else, something to do with the sound he was hearing.

It was getting louder now, still faint, but growing. A larger hissing to it, and a rumble – something to do with a thing his father had said about the mountains.

The mountains and rain.

It was still louder, a crashing sound to it, and he knew suddenly what it was, what was coming, what was already here.

A flash flood.

The heavy rain had moved on *up* the canyon, but it had kept raining, up into the higher canyons still.

And they all fed this one. This canyon that he was in with the sheep formed a giant bowl to catch water, not just from rain but from other canyons as well, washing down the slopes of the valleys and canyons, filling small streams and all of it, all of the streams, emptied into this one main stream.

Going by right next to the wagon.

He was sitting up and as he reached for the zipper on the bag the first wall of water tore past the wagon.

For a moment he felt relief. The wagon was above the cut bank of the streambed – it stood four or five feet high. And from the sound of it all the water seemed to be roaring past well inside the streambed, easily contained.

But the wagon was on the outside edge of a curve, a

curve made of soft dirt and gravel, and the wall of water hit it, bounced off and away to the side, with tremendous force.

He was up, out of the bag, and opened the small door, caught one glimpse of the water foaming downstream in the starlight, turned to see if the sheep were all right – the dogs had them well up and away from the streambed – when the water cut the dirt away and the bank gave way beneath the wagon.

There was at first a small lurch and John actually looked down at the floor by his feet, as if expecting to see the reason, and then it was gone. The part of the bank supporting the two right wheels of the wagon gave way completely.

The wagon fell sideways, rolling as it went, and landed on its side in the water. John had not completely unloaded the wagon yet and boxes of canned goods tumbled over to the side, making the down-side heavier. The wagon didn't slow when it hit the surface but continued over and down until it was three-fourths of the way over to upside down.

The end wall on the front of the wagon was made up of canvas to keep out wind and rain. It was nothing to a six-foot rip of current moving at thirty miles an hour and popped loose almost instantly.

The giving of the canvas probably saved John's life – although he didn't have time to feel grateful.

When the wagon had tumbled the door-opening end had kicked slightly up and knocked John back into the wagon.

He had time to suck just one breath and he was covered with cans of beef stew and pork and beans and chili and close to a ton of water that had come swirling in around the canvas when the top started under.

He would have drowned there, tangled in his own bedding and food, except that when the surge blew in the end of the wagon it turned the whole inside into something close to a tube.

With the door already open because he had been looking outside there was nothing to stop the water and it blew through the wagon with a large *whushing* sound – John later thought it must have been like getting flushed down a giant toilet – carrying everything that was inside the trailer out the back end.

Including John.

He shot out through the door at nearly current speed – from a dead stop to thirty miles an hour in eight or nine feet – and roared downstream like a runaway train.

As he went through the door his head hit the top – which was now the side – and it momentarily stunned him. This added to the confusion of being suddenly tumbled and he was for a few seconds overcome by vertigo. He had no idea which way was up and he kept pulling and pulling trying to get to the surface only to finally realize that he was swimming down, not up.

The water was not deep and there were no boulders, but there were hundreds of other objects caught in the water. Logs and limbs from trees and gear from the wagon. He kept hitting things, coming up under them. Once he thought he was breaking free only to find that his face was coming up inside heavy, wet cloth and realized he was under his sleeping bag.

He broke loose, caught a breath and then another and was immediately slammed sideways into a bank as the stream curved.

'Ooofff!'

The blow knocked the wind out of him and was followed by another hit as a floating pine snag ran into him and smashed him once more into the bank.

'Get away!' He screamed and kicked at the dead tree as if it were an enemy. The branches tangled around him and he fought savagely for two or three seconds, then realized he could simply push it away. As soon as he drew free of the snag the current took him again and he moved downstream two hundred yards before his clawing hands found an aspen trunk along the edge and he stopped himself.

He hung for a moment getting his breath and strength back, then pulled up onto the bank and dragged himself well away from the rushing water. He felt pummeled, beaten, and he sat curled in a ball with his face on his knees, dazed, still confused.

Something came next to him and he opened one eye to see Jenny standing there. He could just see her face in the darkness and she studied his eyes.

'All right,' he mumbled. 'I'm all right.'

But it was a lie and he knew it and so did Jenny. He wasn't hurt bad physically – bruises and some scratches – but was most definitely not all right.

Jenny sat next to him, leaned against his leg, propped her head on his arm and whined.

'It's all right,' he repeated, dropping his hand to her head and neck and petting her. 'Just a little rest now and it'll be all right . . .'

He closed his eyes.

CHAPTER FIFTEEN

He did not sleep but a kind of rest took him. Sometime later, still before daylight, he heard/felt the water going down again and raised his eyes to see that it dropped almost as fast as it had risen. In seeming minutes it was back to a small, peaceful, meandering stream moving through a meadow in a high mountain park.

Like a snake, he thought – raise and hit and gone. He tried to see his watch but it had been smashed when he blew out of the wagon and didn't work.

It didn't matter. Time didn't matter. Nothing much mattered any longer. He was done – the day had whipped him. One day. The old man had come into this country with two horses and a gun and his own father had taken the herd all summer when he was a boy and John made one day.

One day and he had a dead sheep, an injured dog, and his camp gone. Not just wrecked, but gone somewhere downstream.

Daylight came slowly. John sat and watched the eastern sky over the canyon mouth grow faintly gray, then a little more, then brighter until he could see around him.

He thought of leaving. He thought his saddle must still be where it had been. The wagon had tipped off but the saddle had been sitting on the ground and might still be there. He could saddle Speck or Spud and say to hell with it and ride home.

It would take a long day or a little more and he'd be in his room in dry clothes and everything would be all right.

Except the sheep and the dogs.

Yes, he thought – there was that, wasn't there? He couldn't leave and he couldn't stay and he couldn't do anything right . . .

When it was light enough to see where he was walking so he wouldn't step on a snake he stood, like a rusty hinge opening, and started to make his way barefoot and half naked – he was wearing his pants, which he'd been sleeping in, but no shirt – back to the campsite.

Or where the campsite had been.

The wreckage was complete. His saddle was still there, along with the bridle and rope – and the box of medicine for the dogs and sheep. There were also two boxes of gear and a soaked bag of dog food that he'd taken out of the wagon.

He couldn't even see the wagon at first, not until he'd walked almost to the edge of the stream.

'Ahhh . . .' He thought of about six choice words that Cawley or his dad would have used and wondered why he didn't swear.

The wagon was on its side in the stream, but the streambed was deeper than it had been before. When the flash flood came down it gouged and raked away the bottom and bank to deepen the bed and the wagon had settled over on its side until the top was angled downward and the wheels stuck up in the air.

It looked hopeless.

The stream had dropped back to five or six inches, rambling through a gravel bed, and it seemed that a garbage truck had dumped its load along the bed.

Cans of food, parts of the bedding, paper – the paper seemed incredible, scattered bits by the hundreds and he couldn't think how he could have brought so much paper until he saw that all the cans had lost their labels. The water had washed off all the paper labels and scattered them along the streambed.

Junk, he thought – it just looked like junk. Trash.

My trash.

'And it's all I've got,' he said to Jenny. 'My own private trash . . .'

He went to the saddle. It was wet, as were the saddle blanket and bridle but the sun was well up now and it looked to be a clear day and the things would dry fast. Maybe too fast. He worried that the leather in the saddle would crack if it dried too fast and he pulled it into the shade of the willows.

He picked a flat place near the same willows, out in the sun, and started gathering all that he could find.

The force of water had not only pushed him out of the wagon but virtually everything else.

He crawled inside the overturned wagon and fished

out what was left. The harnesses for Speck and Spud were still there. They had tangled on their hooks and had been held in place. But the collars – the thick, padded collars that went around the horses' necks and took the strain of the load – were both gone.

He put the harnesses – they were very old and well oiled but were made of leather – back in the willows with the saddle to dry slowly.

He found one boot almost immediately, just downstream from the wagon.

'At least,' he said to Jenny, 'I can hop around.'

In a short time he found there was some logic to the destruction. At first look the current had seemed just to flush everything away. But the stream wound severely as it moved through the flat of the meadow and at each turn it had to cut into a bank.

As it cut and was forced to turn the water had dropped much of what it was carrying. The part of each turn where the water surged and was forced around proved to be a treasure trove.

He found most of his lost canned goods and the other boot on the second turn down from the wagon. There was also one sack of dog food. The paper of the bag was soaked through and he feared the dog food would be ruined but the manufacturer had thought to put in a plastic liner and it had not been torn.

His pile grew steadily.

He found two boxes of ammunition but could not find the rifle. It didn't seem possible that the steel of the .30-.30 would let it be taken downstream very far but he combed the streambed for it without success.

The rest of his canned goods – or so it seemed, he couldn't be sure – he found in the second and third bends and the dog food sacks were there as well. One of them had been slashed open by a snag and the dog food that hadn't spilled was soaked.

He carried it carefully to the pile. They could eat it first, wet, and maybe that way he wouldn't lose so much.

The search for food took most of the day. In the middle of the afternoon he stopped to eat. He had found his spoon, but couldn't find the can opener. Still, he had his pocketknife and he went to the pile of canned goods.

Without labels it was a gamble. He picked a short, stout can that he thought would have beef stew – there were many beef stews – and he wound up having a spaghetti and meatball lunch. For dessert he opened a can he thought would have fruit cocktail and it proved to contain stewed tomatoes. He didn't remember packing stewed tomatoes, he didn't even *like* stewed tomatoes, but he ate them and tried without much luck to make believe they tasted like fruit cocktail.

He worked until dark and by then he thought he had everything. Or at least everything there was to find. He'd even found the horse collars, not twenty yards apart hung on snags.

The rifle still eluded him, and the wagon was still in the stream, but there wasn't much else missing. He had a stroke of luck. A tree limb snag had jammed across the streambed a quarter of a mile below the wagon and the branches had formed a mesh net across the flow of water.

His sack of extra clothing and the sleeping bag hung up on the mesh. Had they not caught there, floating as they did, he figured they could have gone to Casper, a couple of hundred miles away.

At dark he set up a crude camp. He had found the plastic bag of matches – Tink had taught him that – and he made a fire. His sleeping bag was still wet but his jacket was dry, as were his clothes, which he'd hung over the willows, and he lay next to the fire and settled back to spend the second night, leaning forward now and then to feed a piece of wood to the fire to keep it going.

He had remembered about the horse – about keeping a horse to hand – and he had Speck tethered to the long rope. She could graze and reach water but she was also close if he needed her.

Spud didn't want to be too far from her so he stayed near camp as well and John listened to them rumble and chew and thought that it must not have been so different when the old man had come with his two horses.

I wonder if he had dogs, John thought dreamily, on the edge of sleep. Nobody ever said if he had a dog with him. Maybe he had a dog or two and maybe he camped right here, right on this spot.

He let sleep take him in fits and starts, dreaming about his father and the old man and two horses and the fire, all mixed together, not really hard sleeping.

At two in the morning, with a sliver of moon starting to show, the coyotes hit the herd.

CHAPTER SIXTEEN

He knew exactly what it was, what the scream-yips meant, and he was on his feet and pulling his still-damp boots on before coming fully awake.

They seemed to be everywhere. They had come to the herd in silence but began 'talking' to each other as soon as they were in position and John sorely missed the rifle.

There was a time – John had heard stories – when coyotes ran alone for the most part. They had been trapped and poisoned down to a small number and there were so few of them that it was very unusual to see more than one. But poisoning had been disallowed because it killed eagles and other birds and trapping wasn't very effective in the open prairies.

The end result was that coyotes, for as long as John's life and longer, had been packing up. It wasn't two or three of them here and there, but large packs that formed with other packs into whole social orders and when they came upon something to eat – sheep, calves, game, anything – it was gone.

John knew of a cattle rancher in eastern Wyoming who had stood on a hill with binoculars and watched a single group of over forty coyotes – he estimated forty-seven and a man with him thought fifty-two – killing his calves. He had a gun and would shoot but it was half a mile away and the coyotes would just move a bit and start tearing at the calves again. One or two of them would snap at the cow to keep her busy while others took the calf and when one calf was dead they took another and another.

They were worse with sheep. Sheep were not as tough as cattle and they would rip an ear off a sheep or tear the nose open on a lamb and they would die of shock. The coyotes' favorite place to hit was the rear end, especially the udders on the ewes, and they would tear and go, tear and go, all night or until stopped.

John bridled Speck as fast as he could, untied her, and threw a leg over her without a blanket or the saddle. There was very little time and almost nothing he could do without a gun.

He had heard all the arguments on both sides – for the coyotes and against them. All the ranchers had. And in a way John liked them. They were so smart and had learned to live with man so easily that he had to respect them. But the truth was a pack of coyotes hitting a sheep herd didn't know anything about all the arguments. The sheep were there, they were handy, they were slow and tasted good and that was that. It was a slaughter.

Once a pack had come down to the ranch and hit the herd during lambing – right in back of the lambing barn.

It had been a disaster. There couldn't have been five coyotes in the pack but they tore and chewed and killed forty-one sheep, all ewes waiting to have lambs, in less than two hours at night. They ate none, just hit and ran, tearing and biting and killing them by shock.

John gave Speck heels and she tore off across the meadow around the sheep. The dogs were trying to defend the herd, and could to an extent save them. But when a pack hit they came from different directions and the dogs couldn't stop them all.

The yipping and screaming grew louder, more intense. It sounded like a dozen or more but John knew it could be as few as three or four. Their noise was deceptive.

His eyes were already accustomed to the darkness and he could see the gray field of sheep backs easily, see the disturbances on the off-side of the herd, and he aimed Speck for the first spot.

Sheep were milling and running away and he saw Pete running across sheep to get to the same place and he felt Speck lock on as she saw where he wanted to go.

She ran low and along the ground, smoothly, and before they'd gone fifty yards he saw the coyotes.

There were two of them, both pulling at the rear of a young ewe. She was blatting and going down backward and John ran over them.

Or tried to – they saw the horse coming well ahead of any danger and both of them vanished like fog into the night.

Still farther around the herd he saw another place. There was no time to check on the ewe. He heeled Speck and aimed her and she tore off again, this time with such force he had to hang on to her mane to keep from sliding off over her rump.

Two more coyotes had another ewe. This time she was old and they'd torn her ears off and one of them had her by the nose and Speck nearly got that one because he didn't want to let go. The little mare picked up speed as she approached and the coyote missed getting crushed by less than a foot. Billy had come in from the other side and he got a mouthful of fur as the coyote went by.

Then they were gone.

And except for the milling of the frightened sheep and the sound of the wounded one bleating in pain there was nothing.

For one, almost two minutes.

Then in a slightly different location, not far from the first, the sheep started milling and running in circles and John kneed Speck around and let her go and two coyotes – probably the same first two – were taking another ewe. They had been after her lamb but she had tried to protect it and they had taken her instead.

This time Speck was on them sooner, and so was Jenny, coming from slightly around the herd, and the ewe suffered almost no damage except for a couple of cuts in her shoulder. John could see the blood in the moonlight and dismounted to make certain she wasn't hurt badly but as soon as his feet hit the ground he heard commotion from a new place – clear across the herd – and he clambered back on Speck, only half mounted when she leaped into a full run.

He grabbed her mane, pulled himself the rest of the way up, and they arrived just in time to see Peg get a chunk off the end of the tail on a coyote that had grabbed a lamb and was trying to carry it off.

Four, John thought, maybe five or six. But probably four.

A small breather – Speck actually had time for one long pull of air, let it half out – and there was a new blatting of sheep and lambs and they set off again.

It was, John thought, going to be a long night.

CHAPTER SEVENTEEN

It was also a damaging night. By dawn there were three ewes and two lambs dead – all had died of wound shock – and two other ewes he didn't think would make the day. They had tears around their rear ends and they were both down and quiet. Not a good sign.

As soon as it was full day the coyotes made off and he returned to camp, saddled Spud – Speck had run all night and he let her off to rest – and used his rope to pull in the two ewes that were still alive.

He treated them as best he could with salve and pine tar and tied them down in the shade of the willows. Then he ate a surprise can of beef stew – he thought it would be chili this time – and thought of what to do next.

He needed the rifle.

Most of all, he needed that. The coyotes would come back again and again and if they thought he couldn't do anything – which he couldn't – they would work in the daylight as well. He needed some way to stop them. He needed the rifle.

When he was done eating he took his boots off and stripped to his shorts and went again to the streambed. He started at the wagon and worked downstream carefully, studying the gravel bottom inch by inch.

It did no good. He went to the snag that had held his bedding and well beyond, then turned and came back but there was no sign of the rifle.

'Well – that's it.' He put his clothes back on and turned to look at the next problem.

The wagon.

It lay on its side in the stream. It seemed to be a broken thing but when he looked more closely at it there wasn't any severe damage. The curved hoops that had held the canvas top in place were made of thin pipe and they had bent but they could be straightened again.

The problem was that the wagon had rolled over. He'd have to bring it back upright somehow and then pull it out of the stream.

For a moment he couldn't think how to get it upright. He moved into the stream again – he was getting sick of taking his boots off and putting them back on – and heaved on the wagon but it didn't move. The sand-and-gravel bottom seemed to suck it down and even when he used a heavy tree limb the flood had brought down for a lever the wagon didn't budge.

He moved to the bank again, let the sun dry his feet, and studied the wagon. If he could move it sideways, pull it from the side . . .

He saw the answer. He could use Speck and Spud to pull it back on its wheels from the side.

He went into the willows. The harnesses were damp but had dried enough to stiffen slightly and he worked them with his hands to loosen them a bit. The collars were still soaked but they would work.

He caught Speck – Spud was already on a long picket – and harnessed them. Speck jumped around a bit until she remembered she'd worn the harness to pull the wagon for three days. Spud just looked around at the straps and chains and seemed to shrug.

How to hook them to the side of the wagon was the hard part.

The tongue and doubletree were still attached to the front of the wagon and John went back into the stream and looked at them. The doubletree – the crosspiece the horses actually pulled on – was held to the tongue and wagon by a single drop-pin. It was wedged in but he used a rock from the stream bottom and pounded it out. This gave him the doubletree and the two singletrees to use to hook to the horses.

He brought their trace chains back to the hooks on the doubletree and hooked the two horses up without a tongue between them and left the doubletree lying on the ground.

The horses had been cow pony-trained to stand any-time their reins were left to hang and they waited, swishing their tails to keep the flies moving.

John uncoiled his lariat and threw the end over the top of the wagon. On the backside he pulled the rope down and tied it through a hole in the boards on the side of the wagon. The boards were bolted in place and strong but time had opened small holes here and there as they shrunk or worked at each other and he found a hole just big enough for the rope end.

With the rope over the wagon and tied to the side it ended just at the shoreline.

He picked up the doubletree and pulled backward on it.

'Back, back.' He tried to make his voice low, the way his father's voice would sound. The horses seemed to respond better to a low voice – or maybe just to his father's voice.

Spud and Speck backed in tiny little steps, fidgeting at the chains hanging by their legs as they worked backward.

He let them make their own way, pulling and saying 'Back, back' in the low voice until at last they had come far enough. The hole through the middle of the doubletree was just over the rope and he pushed the end through and tied it.

'There,' he said, standing. 'Now we snort and go.'

He went to the front of the horses and brought them forward slowly until the rope was snug, hanging in the air from the wagon up to the doubletree.

He'd seen his father use a team of horses once when he was very small to pull some tree roots out of the ground and he remembered it now. His father had stood off to the side of the team a bit, not in front and not behind where he could get caught by the end of the chain – in John's case the rope – if the pull snapped it.

John moved to the side, held Speck's bridle strap in his hand and clicked with his tongue.

'Come on, pick it up . . .'

The two horses pulled against the rope, took it tighter

and tighter until it seemed to pull them backward but the wagon didn't move.

'It's supposed to come up,' John mumbled. 'Just come right up.'

He clicked his tongue again, pulled on Speck's bridle and the rope grew tighter still, almost hummed.

And the wagon still didn't move.

'Well, all right . . .' He moved to the rear of Speck and slapped her on the rump.

It was nearly the last thing he did on earth.

The slap wasn't hard but it frightened and startled Speck. She lunged forward, offsetting the doubletree, jerking it sideways. The trace chains flipped into Spud's legs and *he* lunged forward. His sudden movement worsened Speck's fright and in half a second the two of them were nearly crazy, slamming against their harnesses, heaving, driving their back feet into the ground, pulling in an instant jerk that put over a ton of weight on the rope.

Everything happened at once.

There was a great sucking sound and the wagon came up, jumped up off its side upright. But even that didn't release enough of the pressure. The horses were still jerking, lunging forward and all the force of their pull came down to the one smallboard the rope was tied to on the wagon.

It gave. Almost in the same split second as the wagon came up to its wheels the board cracked loose with a sound like gunfire.

John had his back to the wagon still, watching the horses half falling away from their hooves, when he heard the crack. He started to turn, just barely moved to turn and heard a wild, whistling sound and thought the board, the rope and board have broken loose and they're coming at me.

But there was no time to move, to react.

The board hit him across the back of his shoulders like a sledgehammer. He saw something, a spray, out of his nostrils, saw it spray from the wind leaving his lungs because of the force of the blow, saw it as he went down and thought, funny, funny how that sprayed and I didn't even know it was coming.

Funny . . .

All fuzzy and funny how that happened and he was on his knees and then on his face and all the time he thought how funny and fuzzy it was, the spray.

Then he was looking at the dirt and he wasn't thinking anything.

CHAPTER EIGHTEEN

Now, he thought – just that. Now.

Now what? Now to see if I'm really alive. That's next. He tried to think.

He had never really lost consciousness. He knew/felt the horses near him, knew the wagon was upright, heard the sheep in the distance, the rambling gurgle of the stream going by just to his rear.

But his shoulders, his neck, the lower part of his head were alive with pain; throbbing, pounding.

And he could not get air. He pulled, heaved, but it didn't come until just after he passed out a small trickle of air came down, sweet as sugar, and he followed that with another and another and the world stopped swimming.

He raised his head, rolled onto his back.

'God . . .'

New pain pushed out of his shoulders, down his back.

In stages, slowly, he sat up – grunting with the effort

– then over onto his hands and knees, up on his knees and, finally, onto his feet.

Not two minutes had passed since he'd slapped Speck on the rear. Two minutes and a life, a whole life. Had the board caught him six inches higher it would certainly have broken his neck.

And I'd be dead, he thought. Just like that. I would be dead.

He shook his head, took a step. It was wobbly – he nearly fell – but he made it and he took another and felt things loosening up.

He leaned on Speck, patting her neck. Peg and Billy had heard the commotion and had come running from the herd to check on it but went back to the sheep as soon as they saw everything was apparently all right.

They watch, John thought. They watch all things all the time. He hung on Speck's collar for a full minute and felt his strength come back. He left the horses for a moment and went to the stream and splashed water in his face, drank a little.

'So – what have we got?'

He moved to the wagon. It was on its wheels, sitting in the shallow water. The board had snapped out of place just as it came vertical and left it standing. Other than the broken side board he didn't see any real damage.

He moved to the side and looked at where the board had come out, found that it would be easy to cover with a piece of tarp or jam the board back in place, and turned to go back to the horses and bring them around to hook them up and pull the wagon out when something caught his eye.

It was a glint of black metal, down in the water, and he leaned closer to it and found himself looking at the rifle.

It was half buried in gravel, under the water.

'How . . .'

He remembered the wagon going over. The rifle had been leaning against the high side wall and it must have been flipped over against the tarp as the wagon moved, then fallen down through the opening and been under the wagon when it went over.

'It's no wonder I couldn't find it.'

He pulled it out of the water, tipped it so the water could run out of the barrel.

It was mess. Sand and mud came from the barrel and it seemed to have gotten up inside the lever-action housing as well. But there didn't seem to be any major damage. Where the rifle had fallen there had been soft sand and the weight of the side of the wagon coming down on it had merely pushed it down into the sand and not broken anything.

Still, he wouldn't know until he could take it apart and clean it.

That would come later. Now he had the wagon to handle.

And he ran into a snag.

He moved to get the horses and Speck followed easily enough but Spud rebelled. When he got to the edge of the stream he stopped, dead, and didn't want to budge.

'Oh, come on, I've ridden you across streams before. . . .' But even as he said it he knew it wasn't true. The truth was he rode Speck almost all the time and he couldn't honestly remember a time when he had actually ridden Spud into water.

Some horses were like that – were afraid of the water. Cawley told him once it was because they saw the sky in the water, the reflection, and they thought they would fall forever but he'd had a few beers when he said it so John didn't know.

He didn't know that some horses didn't like to go in water and he led Spud again and again to the edge of the water, taking him back in a circle and bringing him down to the water again and each time he stopped.

Speck was in place by the tongue of the wagon and she watched with interest, whickering now and then to them, shaking her head and whether it was this or just John trying again and again Spud finally agreed to do it.

He stepped off the bank carefully, slowly, one foot high out over the water. He brought the foot down hard, clearly thinking the water would be very deep and he would be swimming.

When it stopped in only three or four inches and hit the bottom it jarred Spud's whole body but he still couldn't believe that the water wasn't deep.

He followed John slowly, taking great high steps and slamming his feet down into the water until John – who was by now completely soaked from the splashing – had in position. John was laughing so hard by this time, he had to stop.

'You look ridiculous. . . .'

Finally he had the doubletree back in place and hooked the horses to the wagon and then it proved to be surprisingly easy.

They just walked out of the water – Spud still taking giant steps – and pulled the wagon up into position.

'Up,' John said, walking next to them, 'farther up.'

He pulled the wagon well away from the stream, onto a bit of high, flat ground near some aspens. Then he unhooked the horses, picketed Spud again so he could get to him in a hurry and let Speck run and went to work.

First things first, he decided, and the first thing had to be the sheep. The coyotes would come again tonight, if not sooner – they would stay around the herd and hit as soon as they thought they could get away with it – and he had to handle them.

That meant the rifle and he spread a piece of tarp on the ground and sat to work. It was slow because he had the wrong tools. He had a pair of pliers from the tools in the wagon and a screwdriver-shaped blade on his knife and with these two tools he dismantled the rifle as best he could.

He took the lever off, opened the end of the magazine housing and took the spring and plunger out of the tube – water poured out as it had from the barrel – and he removed every part that he could with his limited tools.

Each piece he placed carefully on a piece of tarp on the ground, in the order that he removed them, trying to keep everything straight in his mind.

Then he used the torn corner of a T-shirt to dry each piece and when that was done he looked for oil.

There was none, but he had Vaseline for the dogs' feet or any other wounds and he placed a thin film of Vaseline on each piece to stop any rust. He used a string to pull a piece of shirt with grease on it through the barrel several times until it shone like a mirror.

When everything was dry and greased he started to rebuild the rifle and did well until he was nearly done and saw a small piece of metal with a screw that had been hidden under a fold of the tarp.

'What . . .?'

It was a piece of the ejector that was screwed into the side of the receiver. He had to remove the bolt and lever and put the small piece in or the spent cartridge cases wouldn't eject.

Finally it was done. It had taken him most of the day but except for some scratches in the blueing the rifle looked almost as good as new.

He worked the lever a few times, easing the hammer down with his thumb, and everything seemed to work right.

Now, he thought, to check it out.

He didn't have a lot of cartridges to waste but he decided to use one to test the rifle.

He pushed the shell into the magazine from the side, then levered it up into the barrel just to make certain everything worked well and fed the shells correctly.

Across the stream, about fifty yards away, there was a mound of dirt left by a badger looking for a place to den up.

John squatted by the wagon and propped the rifle on the tire. He cocked the hammer, took half a breath, let it out and squeezed the trigger.

The recoil slammed back into his shoulder and the crack was stunningly loud in the narrow, quiet confines of the valley. It echoed and reechoed off the sides and filled the whole canyon with sound.

Hundreds of sheep ran, this way and that, and the dogs worked to settle them in. All except for Peg. She came running to John and sat next to him, shaking, and he remembered how much she was afraid of gunfire.

'It's all right, all right. . . .' He petted her, ruffled her ears, and after a moment or two she went back to the herd.

John looked at the target. The bullet had hit within an inch and a half of where he'd been aiming and blown the back of the mound of dirt apart. His father had taught him to shoot, showing him how to hold and squeeze and anytime you could put a bullet within an inch of where you were aiming it would get the job done. John had started to get into shooting the year before, almost too much. He'd spend most of the money he earned on shells and worked day after day on sighting and squeezing until his father had stopped him one morning.

'A rifle is just a tool,' his father had said. 'So you can throw rocks harder than you normally can. Don't ever forget that. It's not anything – just another tool. Like a wrench or a hammer.'

Still, he thought, looking at the mound – it would be different tonight. Much different.

CHAPTER NINETEEN

He spent part of the afternoon cleaning up the camp – he wished he had a hose to clean the mud out of the wagon – and then he rested. The whole night chasing coyotes, the blow he'd taken from the board, and the work of getting the wagon out and clean had exhausted him.

In late afternoon he lay out on his sleeping bag on the ground in the warm sun and lay back to take a nap. He went out like a light.

It was dark when he awakened, dark and cool enough so he could see his breath. The moon was just showing over the eastern rim of the opening to the valley. In his sleep he had pulled the bag over himself and he wanted to close his eyes again and snuggle into the warm bag.

But he heard noise – sheep bleating, running – out on the far side of the herd and knew they were back. The coyotes were there. He couldn't be certain how long they'd been back but the noise snapped him out of the lazy feeling and he jammed his feet into his boots and stood.

He'd tied Spud to the picket rope before sleeping – he would never be without a horse near again – and he bridled and saddled him in less than a minute. He was glad it was Spud because Speck was jumpy when a gun went off. Spud didn't care if you shot right over his head.

There was an empty rifle scabbard tied under the right stirrup of the saddle but he didn't use it. Instead he made certain the rifle was loaded and swung onto Spud and rode with the rifle resting across the sadle.

He let Spud head for the noise on his own and tied a knot in the two reins so they would hang up on the saddle horn and free his hands for the rifle.

It did not take long to get to the trouble. The coyotes were hitting in three places at the same time. The lack of reaction the night before had made them brave, almost cocky, and one of them – a large male – stopped in the moonlight, actually holding a jerking lamb by the back leg, and merely watched as John moved toward him on Spud.

John stopped and raised the rifle. For a second everything hung still, the coyote looking at him, holding the jerking lamb who was bleating for its mother, the horse stopped, little jets of steam from John's breath in the cool night air and he almost didn't shoot.

It was beautiful, too beautiful to end. There would be a crash and then an end to the coyote, an end to the animal standing there. In some way that bothered him. To end an animal, end the life.

But he would shoot, and he knew it. If he did not end the coyote, the coyote would end the lamb. It was that choice.

He squeezed the trigger.

The rifle was thundering – enormously loud in the

night. Spud jumped sideways and in the glare from the fireball coming out the end of the gun John saw that he had held right. He could not see the sights on the rifle but his father had told him to always hold low at night, that people tended to shoot over things in the dark, and John had held on the low edge of the coyote's chest.

The coyote had been hit in the center of the chest and was dead instantly. But it wasn't over. In the half second before John squeezed the trigger the lamb had pulled and the coyote had pulled back and the lamb had been yanked around in front of the coyote. The bullet had gone through the neck of the lamb before killing the coyote and it flopped down on top of the dead coyote.

'No.'

John dismounted and ran to the bodies hoping that it hadn't been as bad as it seemed, that maybe the lamb was just stunned.

But it was dead.

He pulled the lamp from the coyote, carried it off to the side. The mother nudged it with her nose and tried to get it up, bleating in small noises.

'I'm sorry,' John said. 'I didn't mean it. . . .'

Stupid, he thought – stupid. To hesitate. It was the hesitation that had caused the trouble. That half a second of hold let the lamp come around.

But he knew it was more. It was all of it. It was the gun, the killing that caused it. It was wrong, felt wrong, but there was no way around it.

If the sheep were to live, the coyotes had to die.

It was like a law in mathematics. Sheep and coyotes could not be together.

He took the rope from his saddle and looped the noose

around the coyote's neck and used Spud – who was half spooky to be dragging a dead coyote around in the dark – to pull the body of the coyote off into the dark brush and then in a large circle around the herd.

Some ranchers hung the bodies of coyotes on fence posts and let them mummify there, and swore that it helped keep others away. John couldn't bring himself to leave the body around but he thought the dead smell might help and after he'd circled the entire herd he pulled the body into some brush and buried it in a shallow trench, covering it with sticks and rocks.

He carried the body of the lamb off, heeling Spud in a run to leave the following ewe behind, and buried it on the far side of the streambed in some rocks. The coyotes would get it, he knew, but the rocks might keep them away for a time.

Then he moved back to the herd. He rode around them twice slowly and found to his surprise that all the coyotes had gone, vanished. He thought they would stay even with one gone but apparently the sound of the rifle had done the trick.

After the second round he sat still for a time, watching the sheep in the moonlight.

It's always been like this, he thought. For so long nobody can really remember there have been people watching sheep and protecting them, just like this, in the moonlight.

It was in the Bible. The whole thing about Christmas. That night there were shepherds watching their sheep, close to two thousand years ago.

The same moon. The same stars. The same kind of

animal. He wondered if they had dogs and thought they must have. They couldn't have worked sheep without dogs, he thought, then wondered if they had dogs why dogs hadn't come into the story of Christmas. That whole business should have dogs in it. . . .

He was dozing before he knew it – sitting in the saddle asleep, the rifle across his lap. Spud's head hanging down while he caught a nap as well.

John awakened some time later. He had no idea how long he'd slept. It was still dark and the sheep were still bedded down and the dogs were still taking care of things and the coyotes were still gone.

He wiggled the reins to awaken Spud, who snapped his head up, as if surprised to find he was standing with somebody on his back.

John guided him quietly around the herd back to camp where he unsaddled and picketed Spud in case he needed him.

Then he crawled in his bag, put the rifle close by, and lay back to count stars until he was asleep again.

Which took less than thirty seconds and the last thing he thought was that it's always been like this – always just this way.

CHAPTER TWENTY

Days went by.

On the second day after he'd shot the coyote John found a long, dry willow stick and started carving notches, one for each day. There had been a calendar in the wagon. Tink had put it on the wall. It showed a pretty blond girl holding a horse by the bridle chewing on a piece of straw and it was dated 1959. So it wouldn't have been accurate and it didn't matter anyway since the water had taken it on downstream forever.

He didn't count the days so much as want to keep track of how many he was spending in the camp and when he had fifteen days cut in the stick he stopped one morning and realized that he didn't mind it.

None of it.

He didn't mind being alone. Or not alone, but with the dogs and the sheep and the mountains, as Tink would say it. He had at first missed sound – voices, talking, other people, but it wore away in some manner and now he didn't mind so much.

Birds sang in the morning, the sound of the water running by in the creek was almost like music, and he found himself listening more, hearing more. It was almost as if he was waiting to hear something new, waiting to see something different.

And things had definitely changed around the camp.

He imagined himself to be his great-grandfather, or how he thought the old man must have been, and he tried to do everything the way he thought the old man would have done it.

When he did something, he did it to last and did it right. He set the wagon up well away from the stream, even farther than he had it when he first pulled it out of the water, and he put rocks under the wheels so it couldn't move.

He relashed the tarp to the wagon top, stretched it taut, and tied it so the wind couldn't come through.

The inside of the wagon had been a shambles. The water had gutted it, taking even the iron stove nearly out of the door. He found all the parts and used a smooth stone to pound the worst dents out of the chimney and by the third night he had a cheerful fire going inside to cut the chill of the night air.

The lantern had been tangled in the tarp and was not broken. And the five-gallon container of kerosene had been caught up on a snag by the handle so he had plenty of light.

Within a week the inside of the wagon looked almost orderly. The food was stacked in neat rows – still by guess because all the labels were gone – and the bunk was back in place with the mattress dried, the sleeping bag in a neat roll unless he was airing it outside or getting ready to sleep.

At night the rifle was next to the bed – though the coyotes had not returned – and the last thing he did before going to bed was collect dry kindling, small dry sticks of pine or aspen from the stand of trees along the stream, to make a fire in the morning. These he would put beneath the bed and the first thing in the morning he would reach over, still inside the bag, put the wood in the stove over a small pile of shavings, light the fire and heat coffee in a saucepan to have when he got up.

Coffee.

He smiled when he thought of it. It wasn't real coffee but hot water with a small bit of instant coffee in it, just for color and a tiny amount of flavor.

He didn't like it, didn't really even want it, and certianly didn't need it – but it fit the mornings in some way. So he would put his feet down in his boots and take his cup of 'coffee' to the door and sit on the steps and watch the morning start.

Probably, he thought one morning, just like Tink. And he worried that he was becoming a fourteen-year-old, old man. It stayed in his mind for a couple of days but work soon took its place.

And there was plenty of work.

The dogs could herd the sheep, and run the herd, but when problems occurred they came to John.

The rocks tore their feet up at first. It wasn't that there were major wounds – not after the first time. But their feet would get scuffed and rescuffed in the sharp shale on the sides of the valley until they seemed to be running on raw hamburger.

There was no way to heal them while they were running and no way they would stay in camp unless they were forced to stay. What he finally did was work a roster and two dogs would work the herd – a male and a female working in teams – while he tied the other two to the wagon with bits of rope. He would rub ointment on the feet of the two who were 'resting' by the wagon – they hated it and wanted to be with the herd – and it worked to switch dogs every two days. Their feet healed amazingly fast and by the second day they were tough and pliable enough to run.

Which meant the sheep had to be herded by only two dogs.

Sheep, he thought, lived up to the reputation of not being terribly smart. Two dogs were not enough to move them when the grass began to get chewed down in a particular spot – which took only hours. The outside edges of the flock would move but that often meant that the inside area would only have prechewed grass to nibble on and it wasn't as good as the fresh, longer grass. And they wouldn't move on their own but would just stay in the center of the herd, eating the poor grass.

And so they had to be moved.

But two dogs couldn't quite get it done. The sheep would start to move, then filter back around the dogs and go to nibbling again.

John would take Speck or Spud – whichever horse was on duty that day – and ride up to help the dogs. He would work back and forth across the rear of the herd and yell and wave his arms to get them going.

'Huh! Huh!' He made a low, guttural sound, almost a bark, and by the tenth day he noticed that the sheep were maybe a little smarter than he thought.

They watched him and if they saw him riding up from the wagon and the dogs started to move the they would take off on their own before John actually rode close enough to make them move.

The next time he tried it he just saddled the horse and climbed into the saddle and yelled 'Huh!' without leaving the camp area.

The sheep moved, or started to move, and the dogs kept them going until they were all in new grass. And the day after that John didn't saddle up but just walked to the edge of the camp and waved his arms and yelled.

And it worked.

They looked like a huge gray carpet sliding sideways.

'Huh! Huh!'

And they slid sideways on the side of the valley wall, fully half a mile from John, and then Billy and Jenny, the two dogs working the herd, kept them moving until nearly all the sheep were in new grass.

'Like magic,' John said. Four days later he noticed that they started to move before he yelled and realized they were responding to his arm movements. The next morning when it was time to move them to new grass he merely walked to the side of the camp, faced the sheep, and waved his arm.

Over they went.

Six thousand sheep and lambs, one wave.

'Tink must have known this,' he said, watching them move. 'And he never said a word. . . .'

There were many things his father, Cawley, or Tink had not told him. It wasn't that they were holding back on him so much as he hadn't asked and they might not have known how to say things if he had asked.

Everything was so beautiful it seemed to be not real, almost a movie. He had always had what he called 'pretty country' around him. Raised on the Barron ranch made it automatic.

But it was different here.

Down on the ranch there was outside interference. Man-made things were always around. And he liked them, and thought some of them were nice to look at. His saddle, for instance – something about the deep, rich brown of the oiled leather made it seem that he could see down inside it.

But here it was all . . . clean, clear. Just beauty. The mountains rose on both sides and at the far end of the valley, just shot up, and always looked different. He could look at them for ten minutes, look down, take a step, take a breath and look again and they were all different, all new.

Clouds, high giants of white, slashing storms – they were always new and changed while he watched and their beauty matched the mountains.

Matched all of it.

By the end of three weeks things had reversed and he decided one afternoon to try and find what *wasn't* beautiful.

He was sitting on the side of the stream and had his pants rolled up and his bare feet in the water and he looked around and thought of the last three weeks and tried to think of something that *wasn't* beautiful.

And he couldn't.

Maybe the coyotes, the one that grabbed the lamb – but that was part of it as well, part of the beauty. Even that.

His toes.

He looked down at his toes and smiled and nodded.

His big toes were ugly.

Really ugly.

In all of this, he thought, in all of this country it's my big toes. I've got the ugliest toes in the world.

He wiggled them and slammed his feet together like a seal flapping its flippers and lay back and laughed until Jenny – Jenny and Pete were tied to the wagon for their foot-off day – looked at him and whined, thinking he was crazy.

'It's my toes,' he said, turning to her. Pete wagged his tail but Jenny studied his face. 'They're ugly. Man, I've got ugly toes.'

And, of course, he thought, they didn't get it. Dogs don't think about ugly toes. And that set him off again and for the rest of the day, every time he looked down and saw his boots he would think of his toes and smile.

That night the bear hit and he didn't think he would ever smile again.

CHAPTER TWENTY-ONE

He had no idea what it was when he heard the noise and rolled out of the bunk.

He was ready now, always ready to hit the ground running. His feet dropped into the tops of his boots and he pulled them on – he didn't take time for socks – and his left hand automatically grabbed the rifle and he was at the door and outside before his mind really had time to kick into gear.

There was no moon and it was the middle of the night. Flashlight, he thought – I should have a flashlight. He thought momentarily of taking time to light the lantern but decided it would take too long.

Noise.

Something had awakened him. What?

There. It was high in the herd. His eyes were already accustomed to the darkness and in the faint light provided by the stars he could see the sheep up on the side of the valley.

Something was in them. They were scattering and running in all directions and he thought for a moment it was the coyotes, that they had come back.

Then he heard a new sound. A bellowed growl – very deep, guttural, almost human, if a human could get low enough.

On top of the growl he heard a scream of pain from one of the dogs and he was on Speck and riding, bareback, the rifle in one hand and his other tangled in the mane to hang on.

He didn't have time to bridle her and he steered with his knees at first. But she knew probably better than he did where she had to go and inside three leaps she was moving at a lined-out full gallop.

John let himself move with her, felt her slide over the ground.

It was too dark to see anything but shapes. The light color of the wool on the sheep made them relatively easy to see, and the white patches on the dogs made them show a bit. He saw them running, moving back and forth, trying to get at something but whatever it was did not show until he was nearly upon it.

It was a black bear, still down on all fours, swinging around to hit at the dogs. There were three dogs up and trying to dash in and snap the bear on the flank. One dog was down and off to the side – John could just see it against the ground.

There were dead sheep everywhere. He didn't count, didn't even think of it, but they were scattered around and in some cases lying one on top of another.

Everything happened at once. Not just seemed to –

everything happened exactly at the same time.

Speck smelled/saw/heard and recognized the bear just as two more leaps would have taken her right on top of it.

She turned sideways. Didn't pivot, but suddenly went from a horse racing one direction to a horse racing another. It was too fast for John. He had raised the rifle, holding on the center of the black mass – a darker place in the dark night – and Speck turned just as he squeezed the trigger, still at a full run. The gun was unbelievably loud – cracked the night open in a flash-sound. He shot at least a foot wide of the bear.

Without a saddle he couldn't stay on and as she turned and he fired he was at the same instant alone in the air, floating, floating it seemed forever.

He was heading directly for the bear.

He had time for thoughts. The rifle, he thought – if I could work the lever and maybe get the barrel down I could get another shot in before . . .

It was too late. The thought came, hung as he hung in the air, and ended as he landed spread-eagle full on top of the bear.

Everything ended when he landed on the bear. He had seen them before, seen them in the mountains, and knew they could take a terrible toll of sheep. But he had always thought of them as almost cute, like pets, and slow and plodding.

He could not believe how fast this bear moved. He wasn't a large bear – perhaps three hundred pounds – but he was a very mad bear. All he wanted was a few sheep and dogs had come from all directions, snapping at him, and then a horse came out of the night and nearly ran over him and somebody shot at him and then that same somebody flew through the air and landed on him.

He seemed to turn inside his skin, shifted beneath John, rolled and came to his back legs just as John landed, half on his feet.

The bear swung sideways with its right paw. One sweeping hook and it caught John on the left shoulder.

'Ooofff!'

He'd never been hit so hard. Even getting kicked by a horse in the stomach had not been this hard.

He almost literally flew sideways and all still at once, almost at once. Off the horse, the rifle shot, onto the bear, knocked sideways all in less than a second.

A ball, he thought. He'll come after me, try to finish me. Roll in a ball and try to get through it.

But the bear didn't come.

Except for Peg, who was on the ground, the dogs were still there and when he rose to hit John they came in on him. Billy got a mouthful of rump, tore hair out, and went back in. Pete and Jenny took the sides and as the bear wheeled to get one, another came in, snapping, to dance out; and in the spinning to get one dog and then another, the bear forgot John and the sheep. He lowered and backed away, cuffing at the dogs until he could detach from everything and then he moved off into the darkness and was gone.

He left carnage. Dead sheep were everywhere, Peg was down and John was driven into the ground against a small hummock of dirt.

Like a fence post, he thought, or tried to think. He drove me in like a fence post.

He couldn't believe the bear was gone, couldn't believe

he was still alive, couldn't believe his brain still worked. It was like getting hit by a car, he thought – a car moving about sixty. Just wham, and I'm gone.

He was on his right side, his face speared into the dirt, and he rolled onto his back. There was a numbing jolt from his left shoulder and it seemed to pop and he realized the blow had partially dislocated it and he'd moved it back into position when he rolled.

He wanted to scream. It felt like somebody had driven a spike into his shoulder joint.

John lay on his back for a moment, his breath coming in quick pants while the pain rose and fell and finally dropped enough so he could think straight again.

He had been certain the bear would come at him, take him, and he was surprised when it didn't.

John rolled forward, grabbed his shoulder, and held it in place.

Speck had gone off a bit and was standing. He could just see her in the darkness.

Peg, he thought – Peg was down. It was Peg.

He rose to his knees, stood. The gun – he needed to find the rifle. The bear might still be there, waiting to run over him.

His legs were rubbery but they worked and he walked back to where he'd come off the horse. The rifle was there but it took some seeing and he had to lean to finally find it in the dark grass.

He picked it up, worked the lever – there was some sand in it and it grated – and put a fresh shell in the chamber.

Now Peg.

He moved to where she was down. The other dogs had gone back to the herd but several sheep were around the dog on the ground, smelling it and snorting, stamping their feet.

She's dead, he thought. He put his hand to her throat, her chest. It seemed still. No. There. A small movement, she was breathing – just. Short breaths, little tight whuffs of air.

The bear must have hit her, smashed her as he had smashed John. He leaned over Peg and felt her sides, her neck, and then along her back and while he was there, working his hands down the side of her back, he felt wetness.

He couldn't find a wound but the wetness grew and he dug deeper into the fur and then he realized that the wetness was on *top* of his hand and that it was dripping down.

It was from his shoulder.

He was dripping blood from his shoulder where the bear had hit him and with that knowledge the wound shock came and he slowly rolled onto his right side next to Peg and thought, this isn't so bad, not bad at all, and he closed his eyes and decided to take a little nap.

Just lie down next to Peg here, he thought, and take a small nap. It's been such a long day and I'm so tired, so tired, so tired. . . .

CHAPTER TWENTY-TWO

Whining.

Some whining in his ear. No. Not quite. Next to him. A small whine, tiny whimpers.

He opened his eyes and it was still dark. He still held the rifle in his right hand, although it was twisted and jammed into the ground and he was on his back.

How long?

Minutes, hours. Not too long, he thought. Not so very long.

The sound was next to him. Whimpering, soft whining. Peg. She was there and hurt. Yes, there it was, the memory. He'd been hit and was bleeding out of his shoulder and he'd leaned over her, over the dog and dropped.

Peg.

He rose again. Again the weakness came but this time he waited, moved more slowly, and he didn't lose consciousness.

When he was on his knees he reached with his right hand across and felt the shoulder. There was a cut there but it didn't feel so long or deep – not as bad as the pain felt. The cloth of his shirt was damp but the bleeding had stopped.

Peg. Again it came, the small sounds. He had to see about her, get her back down to the wagon.

Everything on his body worked but only with terrible slowness. He stood – like an old hinge creaking open – and looked down at Peg. He could see nothing, no marks on her, could only hear her whining.

He'd have to drag her some way, make a skid, a travois. There was nothing to use nearby – grass and rocks and dead sheep.

Speck was gone, had moved away from the bear smell so she wouldn't be any use until he could catch her and quiet her down. Maybe not even tonight.

All he had was his T-shirt.

He took it off and arranged it on the ground next to Peg's back. With one movement he pulled her onto the spread shirt.

She screamed.

'Easy now, easy . . .'

His voice seemed to help and she settled.

He leaned down and tried to pull with both hands on the shirt and skid Peg along the ground but his left shoulder would not allow him to use his left arm.

He tucked the rifle under his left arm – it would work for that – and used his right hand on the T-shirt and pulled Peg along the ground.

It was slow moving. If he moved fast, or tried to move

fast the whining increased and Peg obviously had greater pain. So he had to move carefully, skidding her over the ground, and that was hard because he had to stoop over and the stooping and holding the rifle hurt his shoulder.

They'd come close to half a mile, he and Speck, to run into the bear and it took him the better part of two hours to pull Peg on his shirt back to the wagon.

Dawn was beginning to bring light as he reached the wagon but he brought the lantern out just the same and lighted it and hung it on the side of the wagon.

At first he could find no mark on Peg, no blood. He brought the lantern down close to her and could still see nothing and might not have found it except that his hand brushed her chest as he moved hair to look for blood or a wound.

She screamed again and her head jerked sideways.

Inside, he thought. It's inside. He lowered his fingers gently against her ribs and he felt it.

One of the small back ribs, away from the lungs, had a break. He could actually feel the break. The bear must have swatted her, knocked Peg as it had done to John, and the blow had broken the rib.

And there was nothing he could do.

His father had broken a rib once, and it had been one of the smaller lower ones, and the doctor had told him that even taping wouldn't help much except to keep him from moving the bone.

'And your body will do that as well,' the doctor had said. 'If you try to move too much the pain will stop you.'

It was the same here. He could tape her but it wouldn't help and she didn't seem to want to move very much anyway. He couldn't get her up into the wagon without lifting her and even if he could – he didn't think his shoulder would let him – it would move her rib bone and the pain would be terrible.

He used dry grass and made a thick bed back beneath the wagon and put a pan of water near the bed and another of food. Then he pulled Peg onto the bed and left her there, still on his torn T-shirt.

In all of this he had not looked at his own wound and with Peg settled beneath the wagon he tried to see his shoulder.

Because of the angle it was impossible to get a good look at it. There was a cut there, sideways across the muscle, and it had bled some – there was blood down his arm – but the bleeding had stopped and much of the pain from the cut was gone, though there was still a healthy ache from the joint inside where it had popped out and in.

A mirror – he needed a mirror. And there wasn't one – not within a two-day ride.

It was full daylight now and he went to the stream. In a calm backwater he leaned at an angle and studied the reflection in the water. It wasn't as good as a mirror but he could at least see the wound directly.

It didn't appear deep and seemed to be bruised as much as actually cut but it had to be cleaned.

He had a first-aid kit and he opened it. There were bandages and small scissors and a small bottle of iodine.

It had a little glass dipper to administer drops to a tiny cut. John shook his head. It would take half the bottle.

He set the lid aside on the steps to the wagon, raised his arm to try to flatten the wound, closed his eyes and took a breath and poured iodine from the bottle directly into the cut.

'Eeeeaaaagh!'

He couldn't help it. It was like pouring molten lead into a wound. The beller came out through his teeth and he forced himself to hold the arm up until all the iodine was in the cut and then he put one of the large bandages on it, taping it carefully. He dug in his bag in the wagon and found a shirt and put it on gently, easing his bad arm into the sleeve. The arm hurt when it hung down straight so he used a strip cut from the edge of the tarp to make a loose sling to hold it when he didn't actually need it.

'So,' he said when he was finally done. 'So now what?'

The sheep, he thought. He had to see to the sheep. The bear had done damage there, torn at them, and he should have taken care of them first. No, the horse. Speck was still up there around – but he hadn't saddled her or bridled her so she could just graze. The gun. First the rifle. If the bear came back he needed that and it was jammed with sand and dirt.

He spread the piece of tarp and again disassembled and cleaned the .30-.30 until it worked like new. He used the corner of his shirt to wipe each cartridge bfore reloading it in the tube magazine and when he was finished with the rifle he carried it in his right hand and went to Speck.

She was still spooky – although it had been five or six hours now since the bear – and she moved away from him when she saw the rifle.

He hid it in back of his leg until he had her halter and she couldn't run.

'It's all right, all right now. . . .' He talked to her while he petted her neck and examined her. He had worried that the bear had perhaps hit her as well but she was fine and in moments had settled enough to nuzzle him against the stomach.

He rubbed her neck and let her go back to grazing and moved to where the bear had hit.

'War,' he said when he got there, speaking aloud without meaning to. 'War must be this way.'

The bear had been horribly, unbelievably destructive. Several sheep were still alive but one of them was wounded so terribly that John shot it. It had been broken almost in half, struck from the top with such force that it had almost literally been snapped into two pieces.

Dead sheep were everywhere. The bear must have run straight into them, striking left and right and they had been jammed together and hadn't been able to get away. One sheep was ripped pretty badly down the side and he started to shoot her as well. He had the hammer back on the rifle and the rifle to the ewe's head and he stopped.

'No. No more.'

The rip had opened the side for close to a foot and he could see the membrane that held the intestines in, and could see the intestines dimly through the membrane and it didn't seem possible that the sheep could live.

'I'll have to get you down to the wagon,' he told her. 'And sew on it. . . .'

While he was wondering how to move the sheep – it seemed sure to kill her if he moved her – the ewe walked off and started eating as calm as if nothing was wrong with her.

'So we'll go slow,' he said. He walked in back of her

and let her make her own speed, moving her left and right, until he had her near the wagon. There he found some twine and tied her.

Sewing the cut was both harder and easier than he thought it would be. It was hard because he had trouble starting. He found the curved needle and a package of sterilized thread and poured disinfectant on the cut. But making himself push the needle through the skin, actually push it through, was hard – the skin hung and the needle didn't go through easily and he had to push harder and harder and finally it broke through.

For one stitch. All that for one small hole. Then he had to push it through the second side and pull the two ends together and tie it in a knot and pull the two sides of the cut together.

Puuuullll them, he thought, tightening the thread. He winced as he did, watching the skin slide back over the membrane, but the ewe stood quietly and seemed not to notice him working on her.

It became easier on the second stitch and by the time he'd finished – twenty stitches – he was moving right along.

The cut pulled together well and when he was done he put pine tar on top of it to keep the flies off. He thought of letting her go but he worried that she would roll on it or get hit by another sheep so he kept her tied with the twine.

When he was done with the ewe he checked on Peg again. She'd been drinking water and he thought she'd eaten some from the pan, or at least nuzzled the food around.

There was still much to do. He caught and saddled Spud and went back to the war zone – as he thought of it. Sixteen dead sheep he counted. The bear had gone crazy. He used his rope and Spud and dragged the sheep bodies, two at a time, three-quarters of a mile from the herd into a dry wash on the side of the valley floor.

Buzzards would come, and the coyotes would come back – he hoped they would leave the herd alone and just clean up the dead ones – and in a few days there would be nothing but bones.

But he hated it, hated the death of it, and when he pulled the last carcass into the wash and saw the mess he thought of films he'd seen on television of mass graves in war and it looked the same to him. The bodies lay in a pile, flopped one on another and it was easy to see how it could be something else other than sheep, could be humans.

He was relieved to turn away, back to the camp, back to sanity.

CHAPTER TWENTY-THREE

He wasn't sure when he saw the difference in himself, or when he started to see it, but a month had gone, then another week, and he wasn't the same any longer.

The camp seemed to be running by itself. He had a ritual. Up just before light, get a fire in the stove, make coffee – he was still drinking it weak and wished he had some tea – and sit on the steps of the trailer and watch the sun come up.

He had never done any of this before – sit and relax and meditate – and now he did it and he would think while he was doing it. Not of work, or what had to be done that day, but just let his mind go and think. Once he thought of his mother, and missed her though he hadn't really known her, and another day of Tink. And again of Cawley and one morning of the girl in the car when he was at the highway.

With sunup he would saddle the horse he was going to use for the day and slide the rifle into the scabbard and move out to check the herd to see if they had weathered the night all right.

The bear never came back. The coyotes did. They cleaned up the dead sheep and then tried the herd again one night but he shot near one – he'd been trying to hit it and shot wide – and they had all disappeared and he hadn't seen them since.

But sometimes the dogs would become too enthusiastic and keep them in such a tight herd that the inner ones didn't get to good grass and John would use his horse to break them open and spread them out.

All around the herd, looking for bear tracks, then back to the wagon to make breakfast – some mystery meal from a can without a label – and straighten the camp, which really only took a few minutes. He put the sleeping bag out to air, washed any dirty socks or other clothing out in the stream, gathered enough driftwood for the stove for the next day or two and dried it beneath the wagon, put ointment on the feet of the two dogs he kept tied to the wagon, rolled the tarp up on the wagon to let fresh air breeze through (unless it was raining), and then it was lunch. Another mystery meal – he was amazed at how often he would guess wrong – and after lunch check the herd again.

All ordered and neat and correct and just falling from one day to the next. He kept a count of them, made the marks in the wagon, but he did not miss home, did not miss anything. It wasn't that he wanted to be alone, or that he wanted to be here – he didn't want anything.

A horse, he thought, and the dogs and the sheep and the mountains. That's all he wanted. Or seemed to need.

Just like Tink had said.

But there came a day, when he had forty-seven days marked in the wagon, he was coming from the afternoon check on the herd and he looked back, down the canyon, and far off saw a figure on a horse emerge from the streambed cut, followed by another horse, a pack-horse, and they came moving slowly up along the stream.

At first it was too far to tell who it was and John sat, watching, letting Speck pick her way back to the wagon.

Then he saw the shoulders, and the way the person was sitting on the horse and knew it was his father and he forgot how he hadn't missed anything, how he liked being alone, how perfect everything was, and slapped Speck on the side of the shoulders with the reins and set her into a flat-out run, heading down the canyon waving his hat and yelling and whooping like a wild thing.

CHAPTER TWENTY-FOUR

They sat by the fire.

His father had brought a canned ham and they had made a large supper of ham and canned baked beans and a loaf of bread his father had wrapped in plastic and kept from drying.

They'd eaten and washed their plates in the stream, each doing his own, and when the meal was finished John made coffee – strong, the way his father liked it – and they sat by the fire on two short pieces of wood and for a long time they didn't say anything, just watched the flames as evening settled in.

John knew his father hadn't missed anything. He'd seen the herd on the hill and the camp and the two resting dogs and once – John watched him out of the corner of his eye – he seemed to nod and smile to himself.

But they hadn't said much. His father rarely talked a great deal and John found himself strangely shy.

When the talk came, as the darkness came in the mountains, it was quick.

That Tink, he ain't going to die – they cut some on him and did some other treatments and they say he'll be back to work in a month or so,' his father said suddenly, smiling. 'Tough old bird. The way I met your mother was strange. Did I ever tell you?'

It came so fast, slipped in on the end of a sentence, that John almost didn't hear it. He shook his head.

'I was over to Cheyenne on some kind of business – I can't remember what it was – and just as I walked out of a boot-repair place I tripped and went down flat on my face on the sidewalk. Knocked the snot out of me and while I was catching my breath I got up on my hands and knees and I heard this voice say:

' "Do you know any other tricks?" And I turned over and there she was, standing above me. The light was coming through her hair and I'd never seen anything that pretty, not even close. I stood up and I knew I was going to marry her. I didn't know her name nor nothing – still don't know much – but I knew by god I was going to marry her if I had to move a mountain to do it and I couldn't think of nothing nor do nothing right until I married her nine months and four days after that, to the hour.'

He stopped just as suddenly as he had started and took a long pull of hot coffee and John almost stared at him. He'd never heard his father say more than a few words at a time and to hear him string them all together, talk about something that had happened, was a complete surprise.

And it wasn't over.

'You take on a lot about the old man,' his father said abruptly. 'That might be good or it might be not so good, depending, and I thought you ought to know some about him and the way he really was before you got to where you were trying to be – well, it just might be better if you know.' He took some more coffee, drained the cup, and chewed on the grounds before swallowing them and pouring a new cup.

'Reason I ain't said anything before is that it wasn't time.' He paused and looked around the camp, out in the coming darkness at the herd and the mountains and maybe something beyond the mountains. 'Now it's time.'

He put the coffee down and picked up a stick and began to whittle on it with his pocketknife, not making anything. John watched the curls of wood come off with the knife. Soft curls, colored like honey, falling off the knife into the fire to flare up and light his face and he sighed and spoke without looking up.

'Some people started that business about the old man being a cowboy and how he came out here with nothing but his gun and two horses and all that. Some of that is true but most of it . . . well, it's said a lot different than it really ran.

'He come out here with a gun, for sure, and some horses – probably a whole herd of 'em – and some cows. But he wasn't alone. There was a hand with him, name of Lincoln – Smiley Lincoln, they called him – and they was partners, or had been partners before that. Some of the details are fuzzy but it was said they rode out here together and took the spread as partners.'

'But I thought he was alone,' John said. 'Everybody said he came out alone. . . .'

'It was what he said, not everybody else – just what

the old man said. *He* said he did it alone. But there were other people to come along and they saw things differently. The other people said they was partners, the old man and Smiley, and settled the spread together and then the old man wanted it all for himself.'

He stopped talking for a moment. The knife kept peeling curlings off the wood, dropping them in the fire and John watched them. Drop, flare, drop, flare. He didn't know what to think.

'So there come a day when the old man just said he was taking it, the spread, all for himself, and when Smiley tried to argue the old man up and shot him.'

'What?'

His father nodded. 'That's right. He shot and killed Smiley. He said later that Smiley took a rifle out of his saddle scabbard and started to point it at him but there were others who said Smiley was shot in the back. After he shot him the old man dragged Smiley up into a gully and covered him with rocks. . . .'

John thought of the coyotes and sheep, how he had dragged them away. 'But . . .'

'. . . and that's probably the truth of it all. He was mean, the old man, spit mean, and there were too many people who spoke of what had really happened to let the old man's story stand.'

'He was a murderer?'

His father nodded. 'That's about the size of it.'

'So all this . . . this land that he took, the spread – he took it all by killing his partner?'

His father nodded again but said nothing.

'Why didn't you tell me before?'

'You were using it to live.' His father sighed. 'You didn't know the bad parts and you were using the good parts of the story to live and it seemed wrong to cut that down when you were using it. But now you're getting older and taking things on yourself – here with the sheep and all – and it don't seem like you need that other business anymore. I was . . . worried . . . that you would go too far with it and turn into something like the old man.'

'He was a murderer?' John asked again. 'He just shot his partner? Why wasn't he hung?'

'Things were different then. Or sort of different. Nobody saw it so they couldn't prove it and then there were many who were afraid to speak up. He shot several men. Seems he didn't need much of an excuse to shoot somebody. Your momma, she hated him – the memory of him.'

'Did she know him?'

'No. Except for Tink none of us did. I saw him once in the old folks' home but I was just a baby. They let him keep his gun there but took the pin out of it so he couldn't shoot anybody. He died with the gun by his bed. They said he died alone. His wife – she was named Emma – she wouldn't go to be with him though she was still alive. People think the ranch was lost to bad debts. It ain't so. That's just another story. It was Emma – she sold it all to the easterners. Sold every bit of it and then gave the money away to a church.'

'Why?'

'She said it was evil. Poison money from a poison place. But that ain't so. A place is just a place. It's as good to live here as it is anywhere – better than some. How it came to be isn't our business. We just live.'

'So that's why we don't own it.'

'Yup.'

'All this time I thought it was just that the family didn't manage it right and lost it. And she sold it.'

'Every square foot. She kept enough to pay for her own nursing home and to bury her and the old man and gave the rest to a church.'

John leaned back. The fire was dying down and he put more wood on it. Out in the night he heard the horses chewing. If they weren't sleeping they were chewing, it seemed. Peg and Billy were tied to the wagon and Peg whined at something in the night, then lay back and slept. She was completely recovered from the bear and worked the herd but had stopped staying out with them when her time was done. She was spoiled and came in to sleep in the wagon. John didn't mind although it bent Jenny's nose a bit and they often growled at each other in the wagon at night.

'I'm sorry about this,' his father said. 'About telling you all this. . . .'

John shook his head. 'It's all right. It's better that I know.'

'I had me a brother.'

John stared at him. He had never heard that his father had a brother. 'I have an uncle?'

His father took a deep breath, let it out. 'No. You *had* an uncle. He took after the old man and turned mean and went to working as a roughneck on some oil rigs down in Oklahoma and another roughneck killed him with a piece of pipe in an oil camp bar.'

'You never said anything about him.'

'He wasn't worth mentioning. He was mean from the get-go – born bad. That's why I told you about the old man. My brother was the same way about him, took to talking about him all the time, had a picture of him. I was getting worried that you might be moving the same way.'

John leaned back and thought about the old man, what he knew of him, and now this new thing. He shook his head. 'I don't think you had to worry. I mean, wouldn't I know if I was mean? And I don't feel mean.'

His father smiled. 'Well – I guess you'd be the first to know.'

'Are there more things about him?' John asked. 'Any good things?'

'Not so many. In fact none. It was said of him that he never did a deal when he didn't come out the best no matter what he had to do. And even when he made money he didn't give any to Emma. He had silver Mexican eagle spurs and she had to make dresses out of feed sacks. He was just bad, that's all. Sometimes they come that way – people. Just come bad.'

For a long time he was silent, the knife still sliding through the wood, and John closed his eyes and tried to feel disappointed and thought that he would have, he would have been sad except for the sheep. And the mountains. And the dogs. And what the past month and more had made him.

'I'm not,' he said quietly, after another long silence, 'like him, I mean. I'm not like him.'

His father nodded. Then he took a breath and started talking again. 'The night you was due to be born it come on to snowing so bad we weren't sure we would get to the hospital. So we set out early and Tink came with us and he had a bunch of rags and I think that's why you didn't come for two more days. Your mother saw Tink sitting next to her in that pickup cab with all those rags he used on sheep when they had lambs and she told me she would wait, thank you, until we got through to Cheyenne even if it took another month.' He laughed. 'Man, you were ugly when you came. Lambs are prettier than people. You were all over gunk and blood and the first thing you did was stick your fist in your mouth and try to eat and they hadn't even cut the cord yet. They let me hold you right away and I could fit you in one hand, my right hand, and your momma, she worried that I would drop you but I never did, never did. . . .'

And he kept talking. John's eyes closed and everything swirled together, the talk and how he looked as a baby and the old man and his father whittling and the fire and the sheep and the dogs and he could not stay awake.

He dozed, up on his elbow, facing the fire, and once when he opened his eyes nothing had changed. His father was still talking, talking about his childhood and a horse he had named Scruffy or Ruffy, it didn't matter, and John dozed again and awakened once more to find his father tucking him into his sleeping bag, as he had when John was a young boy, and leaning down to kiss him on the forehead and John went to sleep smiling, thinking on how nice things could be.

CHAPTER TWENTY-FIVE

It was the next morning.

His father was set for leaving. He'd talked most of the night and still got up early to make a fire and coffee and feed some oats to his horse to get ready for the ride.

The two were silent but it wasn't uncomfortable. John saddled Speck to check on the herd and his father saddled his own horse and joined him.

John showed him where the bear had attacked, how he was working the herd up one side of the valley and back down the other to keep them on fresh grass, how the herd responded to his hand motions.

But at last they were back at the wagon and it was time for his father to go and just then, just at that moment, John didn't want his father to leave. There was some new thing between them, from the talk all night, and he didn't want him to leave and he finally said it.

'I don't want you to leave.'

His father had just finished tightening the pack saddle

on the packhorse and he turned and nodded. 'I feel the same but there's the ranch and Cawley and all.'

They said nothing more about it. His father mounted and caught up the packhorse lead and John mounted Speck and rode with him down the canyon, both of them riding in silence, until they were near the end and John stopped. 'I'd better get back to the herd.'

His father nodded. 'I'll see you in a month or less. . . .'

And he left, went into the small hills and was soon out of sight, gone from the valley, and John waved at where he'd been. Then he turned toward the herd and thought he would miss something now, now because his father wasn't staying with him. There was something special he would miss and he didn't even know what it was and he was halfway back to the wagon when Speck stopped.

'What's the matter with you?'

He nudged her into movement but she hadn't gone twenty feet when she stopped again and this time turned her head and looked back, past John's leg, back down the canyon.

John turned.

Way back at the mouth of the valley where the stream cut through the hills he saw the small figure of his father riding back toward him, picking his way slowly.

John turned Speck and set her into a lined-out run until he swung wide and pulled in next to his father so sharp she settled on her rear.

'I started thinking it wasn't but three weeks till we take the herd down,' his father said. 'And Cawley can handle things down there for three weeks and it's been some time since I spent any time in the haymeadow and there's some things I ain't told you yet.'

John pulled Speck over and fell in beside him, the horses walking and thought: Ain't it funny what makes a person glad? Just to see that little figure riding back with the packhorse in back of it and you could feel all glad.

'Like the time your mother was leading the parade in Cheyenne on a palomino that wasn't good for nothing but show and her pants split? She always did wear them too tight, her pants, and they split like a gunshot and she went right ahead and finished the parade. I found some of that shiny tape and she put that over the split and pretended she was the Queen of Sheba and nobody said a word, not a word. Of course, she could do things like that, your mother. . . .'

Ain't it, John thought again, ain't it just crazy what makes a person glad?

And they rode up the canyon into the haymeadow. And the sheep. And the dogs. And the mountains.

Gary Paulsen
Hatchet

There was almost no light when he opened his eyes again. The darkness of night was thick and for a moment he began to panic ... The world came back. He was still in pain, all-over pain ...

When a thirteen-year-old city boy crash lands into the Canadian wilderness, all he is left with is a hatchet – and the need to survive. From now on he learns everything the hard way ...

'A heart-stopping story ... something beyond adventure.'
Publishers Weekly

'A spellbinding winner.'
Kirkus Reviews

A 1988 NEWBERY HONOR BOOK

Gary Paulsen
Hatchet: The Return

'We want you to do it again ...'

Two years earlier, Brian had been stranded alone in the wilderness for fifty-four days with nothing but a small hatchet. Yet he survived. Now they want him to do it again – to go back into the wilderness so that others can learn the survival techniques that kept him alive. This time he would not be alone. He would have company and equipment. But the violent forces of nature rob Brian of these luxuries, and he finds himself once more isolated and in danger ...